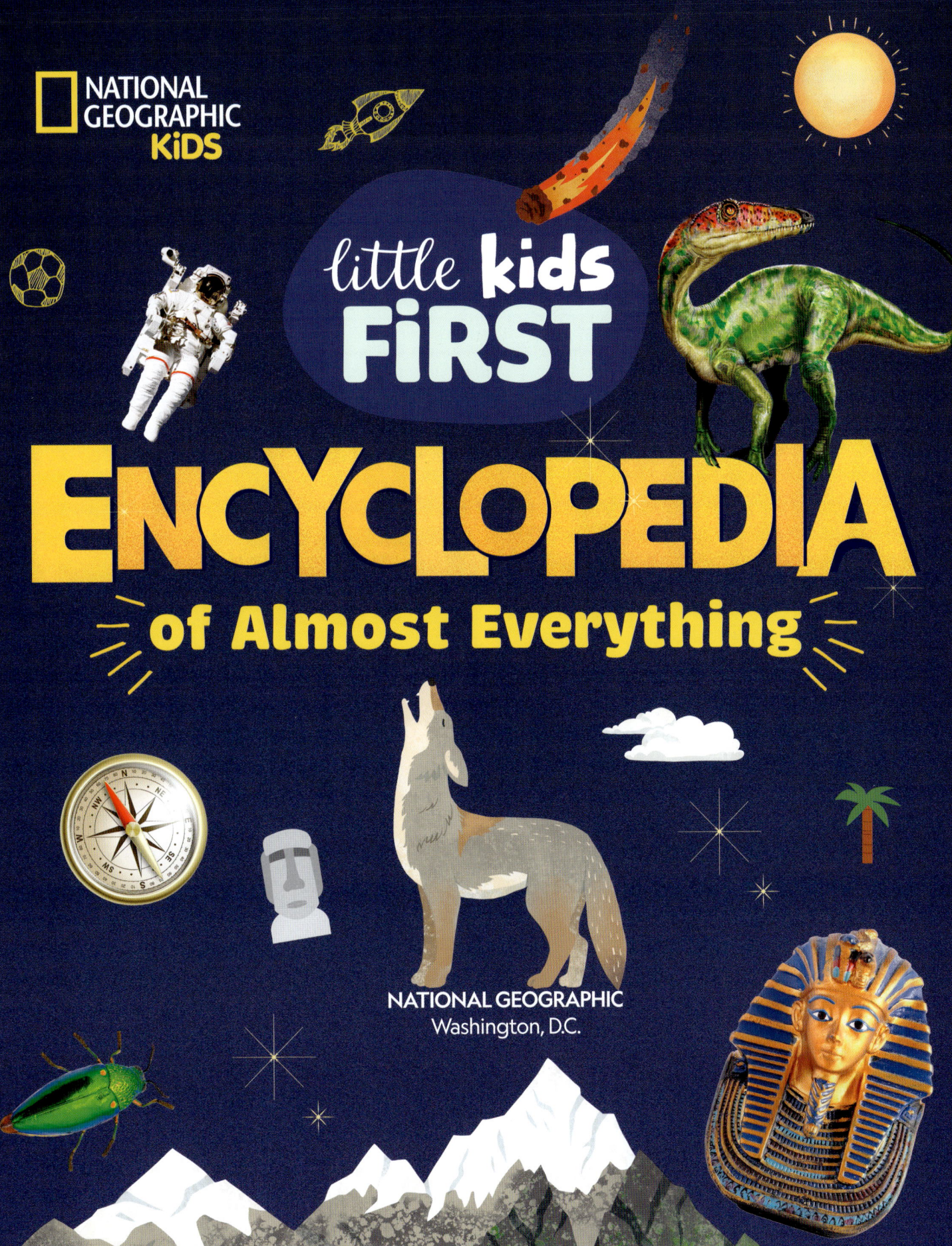

little kids FiRST
ENCYCLOPEDIA
of Almost Everything

NATIONAL GEOGRAPHIC
Washington, D.C.

CONTENTS

CHAPTER 3: BIG WIDE WORLD — 64

CHAPTER 4: FROM THE GROUND UP — 86

CHAPTER 5: CREATURE FEATURE! — 110

CHAPTER 6:
DINO-ROAR!
164

CHAPTER 7:
TIME MACHINE
180

CHAPTER 8:
BRIGHT IDEAS
200

CHAPTER 9: THINGS THAT ZOOM! 222

CHAPTER 10: OUT OF THIS WORLD 238

CHAPTER 1

All About You

What makes you **YOU?** How does your **body work** when you **eat, play,** and **sleep?** Turn the page to find out all about your **busy body,** from the top of your **head** to the **tips** of your **toes!**

9

MEET YOUR BODY

Look at you! Your body is amazing. It is made up of a lot of different parts that work together. When you look in the mirror, what parts can you see?

EARS

Your ears help you hear sounds. Some sounds might be loud. Others are quiet.

MOUTH

You use your mouth to talk and to chew your food.

FINGERS

Your 10 fingers can feel whether something is soft or scratchy, cool or warm. They help you pick up tiny toys or grip a zipper to close your jacket.

Your **teeth** are the **hardest** things in your body.

Your **tongue** is about **three inches** (8 cm) long.

KNUCKLES ▶

EYES

Look! Your eyes help you see the people and things around you.

NOSE

Sniff, sniff! You use your nose to smell things. You breathe through it, too!

HAIR

Your hair keeps your head warm and protects it from sunburn.

Hair **isn't** just on your **head!** There are **tiny hairs** all over your body, even **inside** your **nose** and **ears.**

Your **knuckles** are where your **fingers join** your hands.

ELBOWS

When you eat a snack or wave your hand, your elbows help your arms bend.

KNEES

When you push yourself on a swing or kick a ball, your knees help your legs bend.

LEGS

When you walk, run, jump, or dance, your legs are hard at work.

The **bottom** of your foot is called the **sole.**

FEET

Your feet support the weight of your entire body.

SUPER SKELETON

Your skeleton has more than 200 bones! Bones are hard. They protect your insides and give your body its shape.

Your skull is made up of **22 bones.** Only one, the **lower jaw,** can move. It helps **open** and **close** your mouth.

LOWER JAW

SKULL

Your skull protects your brain.

COLLARBONE

This long bone connects your arms to your body.

HANDS

A human hand has 27 bones.

FEMUR

The thigh bone, or femur, is the longest and strongest bone in the human body.

FEET

Each of your feet has 26 bones.

RIB CAGE

Your rib cage protects your heart, lungs, and liver.

SPINE

Your spine, or backbone, is made up of small bones that are stacked on top of each other. Your spine holds your body upright.

PELVIS

These bones support your spine.

DID YOU KNOW?

Joints are places where bones connect. They allow your body to bend and move. Elbows, knees, wrists, ankles, and hips are all joints.

MIGHTY MUSCLES

Your body has about 600 muscles. These special tissues can tighten and relax, allowing your body to move. When you run, write your name, or chew your food, you can thank your muscles!

Some of your body's **strongest muscles** are in **your jaws.** They help you **chew.**

FACIAL MUSCLES

These muscles in your face help you smile, frown, and make every expression in between.

BICEPS

Your biceps move your arms and help you lift things.

DELTOIDS

These muscles move your shoulders.

HAND MUSCLES

More than 30 muscles help your hand open and close to grab, hold, and move things.

ABDOMINAL MUSCLES

These muscles above your belly button protect your spine and help you keep your balance.

GLUTEUS MAXIMUS

This is a fancy name for the muscles in your bottom.

QUADRICEPS

These big muscles in your legs help you walk, run, and climb.

Tendons connect muscles to bones. When **muscles** move, **bones** move, too.

13

AWESOME ORGANS

There's a lot happening inside your body! Each of your organs has a special job. But they work as a team to keep your body running.

BRAIN

Your brain is the organ in charge! It makes all your other organs and muscles work together.

HEART

Your heart pumps blood through your body.

LIVER

Your liver processes the vitamins from the food you eat and cleans your blood.

STOMACH

Your stomach breaks down your food into a liquid. Then it squeezes that liquid into the small intestine.

INTESTINES

Your small intestine breaks down your food even more. Your large intestine makes poop!

Your skin is your **biggest organ.** It **protects** the rest of your body.

LUNGS

You have two lungs. They help you breathe.

KIDNEYS

Your two kidneys make pee, or urine, the liquid you flush down the toilet!

DIAPHRAGM

This big muscle helps pull air into your lungs when you inhale, or breathe in. It also helps push air out of your lungs when you exhale, or breathe out.

BLADDER

This organ can expand like a balloon to store urine until you go to the bathroom.

RESPIRATORY SYSTEM

When you breathe, you take in oxygen from the air that your body needs. Your nose, mouth, and throat bring the oxygen to your lungs.

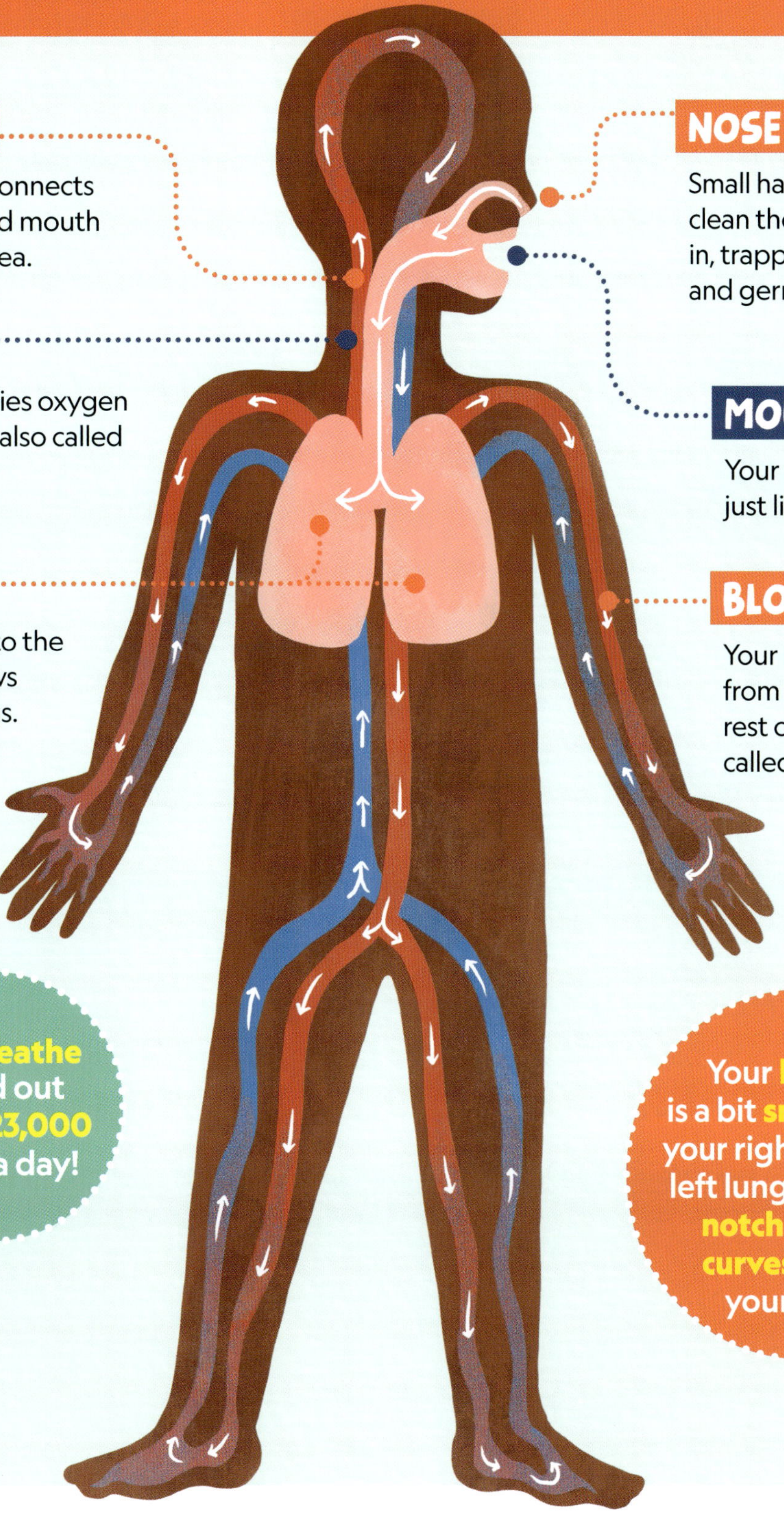

THROAT

Your throat connects your nose and mouth to your trachea.

TRACHEA

This stiff tube carries oxygen to your lungs. It is also called the windpipe.

LUNGS

Oxygen passes into the blood when it flows through your lungs.

NOSE

Small hairs in your nose clean the air you breathe in, trapping dust, pollen, and germs.

MOUTH

Your mouth brings in air just like your nose does.

BLOOD

Your blood carries oxygen from your lungs to the rest of your body in tubes called blood vessels.

You **breathe** in and out about **23,000 times** a day!

Your **left lung** is a bit **smaller** than your right lung. The left lung has a little **notch** where it **curves around** your heart.

15

CIRCULATORY SYSTEM

Your heart pumps blood all around your body. Tubes called blood vessels carry the blood to every part of you.

Your heart **delivers blood** to every part of your body in less than a **minute.**

ARTERIES

Arteries are blood vessels that carry blood away from the heart.

PULMONARY ARTERY

This big artery carries blood from the heart to the lungs, where the blood picks up oxygen.

HEART

Your heart is a muscle that powers your circulatory system. It beats all the time to keep your blood moving.

A doctor uses a **stethoscope** to listen to your **heartbeat.**

VEINS

Veins are blood vessels that carry blood back toward the heart.

AORTA

This big artery divides into small arteries. These carry oxygen-filled blood from the heart to all parts of your body.

DID YOU KNOW?

An adult has about 60,000 miles (96,500 km) of blood vessels. If you could lay them end to end, they would circle Earth more than twice!

Heart

Your heart works hard! The left side pumps oxygen-filled blood to all the parts of your body. The blood then returns to the right side of your heart. The right side pumps the blood to your lungs to get more oxygen. And the cycle begins again!

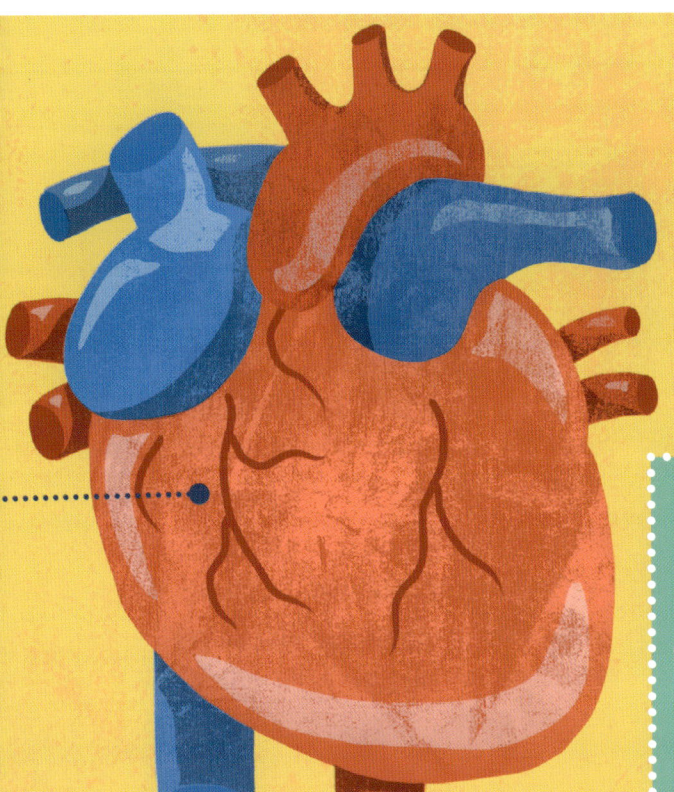

DID YOU KNOW?

Valves in your heart open and shut to allow blood to flow through. As these flaps open and close, they make the sound of your heartbeat.

Countless Cells

Every living thing is made up of teeny-tiny jellylike blobs called cells. Your body is made up of trillions of cells! The many different types of cells in your body have different jobs, but they all need oxygen to work. Your blood's main job is to deliver it to them!

Your **heart** is about the **size** of **your fist.**

◄ BLOOD VESSEL

RED BLOOD CELLS

Red blood cells help carry oxygen through your body.

WHITE BLOOD CELLS

These cells in your blood help fight germs when you get sick.

PLASMA

More than half your blood is made up of this liquid.

DIGESTIVE SYSTEM

What happens to the apple you just ate for lunch? Let's follow that fruit as it moves through your digestive system.

MOUTH

MOUTH

Before you even take your first bite, your digestive system is at work. When you see—or even think about!—that shiny apple, your mouth will make extra saliva, or spit. This slimy stuff coats and helps break down the food you eat, making it easier to swallow.

TEETH

Crunch! You bite into the apple. As you chew, your teeth crush and grind the food so your body can better digest it.

TONGUE

Small organs on your tongue called taste buds help you taste the sweet fruit. Your tongue moves the food to the top of your mouth. Gulp! You swallow.

TONGUE

ESOPHAGUS

The chewed-up apple goes down your esophagus. Muscles in this slippery tube squeeze the food into your stomach.

FOOD

Your **mouth** can make as much as **six cups** (1.4 L) of **saliva** a day!

STOMACH

Your stomach mixes the food with digestive juices. This helps break down food even more.

LARGE INTESTINE

The small intestine carries the soupy mix that was once an apple to the last stop, the large intestine. This organ pushes out the parts of the food your body doesn't need. That's what poop is!

Why Is Poop so Smelly?

Your digestive system has lots of bacteria. These tiny living things help break down your food. This process creates gases that stink.

Poop is mostly made of water.

SMALL INTESTINE

Your stomach empties the food into your small intestine. This twisty tunnel pulls nutrients out of the food. Nutrients give you energy and help you grow.

POOP

Your **small intestine** is the **longest** part of your **digestive system.**

An **empty** stomach is about the **size of a baseball.** But it **stretches** and gets bigger when **food arrives!**

YOUR BEAUTIFUL BRAIN

When it comes to your body, your brain's the boss! It controls everything from the decisions you make to the emotions you feel to the breaths you take. Even when you're asleep, your brain is busy!

Your brain is **wrinkly!** If it were **spread out,** it would be about the size of a **pillowcase.**

CEREBRUM

This is the biggest part of your brain. You make decisions, manage emotions, and store your memories here.

Your brain uses **more** of your body's **energy** than any other organ.

CEREBELLUM

This part of your brain controls movement and balance.

DID YOU KNOW?

An adult brain weighs three pounds (1.4 kg)—about as much as 12 small apples.

BRAIN STEM

The brain stem is in charge of jobs like breathing, swallowing, and controlling your heartbeat.

NERVOUS SYSTEM

Nerves carry messages back and forth between your brain and every part of your body.

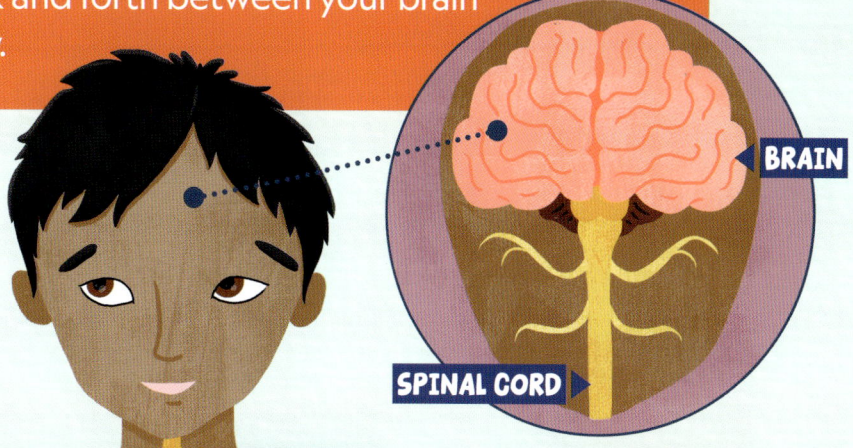

BRAIN

SPINAL CORD

NERVES

Thin and threadlike, nerves run down your spinal cord and branch out to the tips of your fingers and toes.

SPINAL CORD

BODY FUNCTIONS

The nervous system controls jobs that your other organs and systems do, from breathing and sweating to smiling and going to the bathroom.

The **information** from your brain travels **fast!** It can zip along at more than **300 miles** an hour (483 km/h).

LEARNING AND MEMORY

Practicing something—like riding a bike or playing the piano—builds connections in your brain so your body remembers how to do it.

MOVEMENT

Nerves connect your muscles to your brain. When you move, nerves tell your brain which muscles to use.

SUPER SKIN

Skin comes in many different colors, but everyone's skin has the same important jobs. It holds our bodies together and protects everything inside. Your body's biggest organ has a lot to do!

Your skin is **thinnest** on your **eyelids** and **thickest** on your **heels and palms.**

KEEPING COOL

The little drops of water trickling down your face after you run are called sweat. Sweat is your skin's way of keeping you cool.

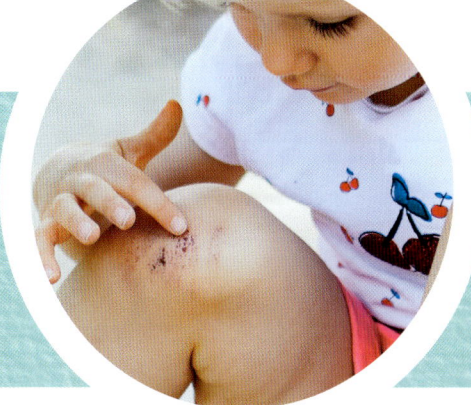

TO THE RESCUE

If you scrape your elbow, your skin quickly works to help you heal. Your skin forms a scab. Under this crusty cover, your skin makes new skin. When the scab falls off, you'll see that the scrape has faded away. All better!

SKIN SAVERS

Your hair and nails are made of keratin. This tough stuff helps protect your skin. The hair on your head saves your scalp from a sunburn. Your nails protect the soft skin on the tips of your fingers and toes.

DID YOU KNOW?

Other animals have body parts made of keratin, too. A porcupine's quills, a turtle's shell, and a rhinoceros's horn are all made of keratin.

Skin Layers

Your skin is made up of three layers.

1. EPIDERMIS

Look at the skin on your hand. That's the top layer, or epidermis, of your skin.

2. DERMIS

You can't see the second layer of your skin. The dermis has blood vessels and nerves. Hair grows from this layer. Sweat is made here, too.

3. HYPODERMIS

The deepest layer is mostly made of fat. This squishy skin keeps you warm and works like a cushion to protect your insides.

Fingerprints

Press your fingers onto an ink pad and then onto a piece of paper. Now look at your fingerprints! No one else in the world has fingerprints that look like yours. But all fingerprints share the same patterns: loops, whorls, and arches. Tiny ridges on your skin create these patterns. The ridges also help us feel and grip things.

LOOP

WHORL

ARCH

FIVE SENSES

Your body has five main ways to get information about the world. These are called senses. They are sight, hearing, smell, taste, and touch.

HEARING

All sounds, from music to dogs barking, are made up of invisible vibrations, or waves. These waves go into your ears, where they make tiny bones jiggle. These bones then send messages to your brain about the sounds around you.

SMELL

Inside your nose are millions of special cells called receptors. Receptors notice and recognize odors. They send signals to your brain, which tells you what you smell: "Yum, popcorn!" or "Pee-ew, stinky socks!"

The **smallest bones** in your body are in your **ears.**

Your **nose** can detect more than **one trillion** different **smells!**

TASTE

Your tongue is covered with about 10,000 little bumps called taste buds. Taste buds can recognize five different flavors: salty, sweet, sour, bitter, and umami (a meaty flavor). Your nose helps, too! Your brain puts tastes and smells together to figure out the flavors of food.

TOUCH

When you touch something, special receptors in your skin send a message to your brain that tells it whether that something is hard or soft, bumpy or smooth, dry or wet, cold or hot.

SIGHT

When light goes into your eyes, special cells turn the light into signals for your brain. Your brain turns the signals into a picture of what you're seeing.

THE IRIS IS THE COLORED PART OF YOUR EYE.

Inside Your Eyes

Your eyes work like a camera, taking pictures of the world around you. Here is how the parts of your eyes work together to help you see.

1 Light first enters your eye through a clear covering called the cornea.

2 Behind the cornea is the pupil. The light moves through the pupil and hits the lens.

3 The lens focuses the light on the retina, at the back of the eyeball.

4 The retina sends your brain a picture of what you're seeing.

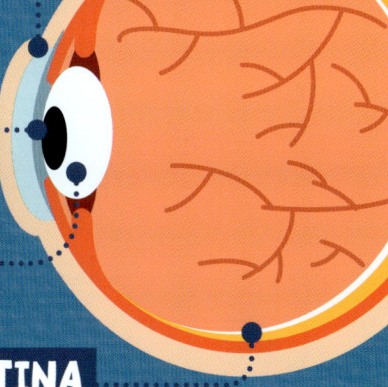

CORNEA

PUPIL

LENS

RETINA

DID YOU KNOW?

An ostrich has the largest eyes of any land animal.

WHOOPS!

We can't always control when our bodies do certain things. But don't worry—they happen to everyone!

YAWNING

Scientists aren't sure why people yawn. It may help wake you up when you are bored or sleepy. Yawning is often contagious—just reading about it might make you yawn!

Other **animals yawn,** too!

GIGGLING

Some parts of your body may be so sensitive that it makes you laugh when another person or thing tickles them.

Most **babies** start **laughing** when they are about **four months** old.

BLUSHING

When you feel embarrassed or extra excited, blood may rush toward your skin's surface. This makes your face feel warm or turn red.

BURPING AND TOOTING

When you eat and drink, you swallow air, too. Air is made of gases. When gas gets trapped inside your body, it finds a way out. Excuse you!

STOMACH GROWLING

When you're hungry, your brain sends messages to your stomach. Your stomach starts to move, making sounds that remind you to eat.

SHIVERING

If you get cold, your body tries to warm itself up. Your muscles shrink and expand very quickly to create heat. This makes you shiver.

SNEEZING

When you breathe in, dust or other teeny-tiny bits in the air make their way into your nose and throat. If your body feels irritated by these particles, you will sneeze to push them out!

Achoo!

Many parts of your body help your nose get rid of dust and other particles in the air. See how your body makes a sneeze.

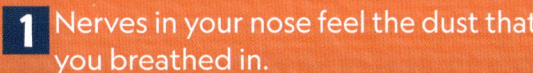

1 Nerves in your nose feel the dust that you breathed in.

2 The nerves send a signal to the sneeze center in your brain.

3 Your brain sends a message to your chest muscles, forcing air out of your lungs.

4 This air rushes out of your nose and mouth. Bless you!

FANTASTIC FOOD

Your body gets energy from food. Eating different kinds of foods gives your body the nutrients it needs to grow.

FIBER

Fruits, vegetables, and whole grains all contain fiber, which helps with digestion to keep your insides clean.

Eating **fruits** and **vegetables** of **different colors** is one way to make sure you are getting a lot of **important vitamins.**

PROTEIN

Meats, beans, dairy, and nuts all have lots of protein. Proteins build strong muscles and help your body heal.

CARBOHYDRATES

These can be found in grains, such as rice and wheat, and in fruits and vegetables. Carbohydrates give your body energy.

FATS

Fats from such things as olive oil, cheese, avocado, nuts, and seeds give you energy and help your body absorb nutrients.

Carrots have important **vitamins** that help with your **eyesight.**

DID YOU KNOW?

Sugary treats can be tasty, but too much sugar can make you feel sick.

VITAMINS AND MINERALS

There are many types of vitamins and minerals found in different foods. These substances help keep you strong and healthy.

ON THE MOVE

Do you like to play ball? Ride your bike? Build cool forts? Work on art projects? Keeping your body busy also keeps it healthy.

SMILE!

Get moving with your favorite activity and feel the good mood coming on! When you're active, your brain creates chemicals called endorphins that can make you happy.

HEALTHY HEART

Like other muscles in your body, your heart gets stronger when you're on the move. Physical activity makes your heart beat faster so that it can quickly pump more blood and oxygen to your moving muscles.

STRONG SKELETON

Exercise makes your bones stronger, too.

LOVE YOUR LUNGS

When you exercise, you breathe faster. Your lungs work harder to make the extra oxygen that your muscles need to move. Over time, your lungs get stronger. Game of tag, anyone?

STRETCH YOURSELF

Exercise can make you more flexible, helping your muscles and joints bend and move more easily.

SLEEP TIGHT

At the end of each day, your body needs a break. Sleep lets your body rest and gets it ready to work and play the next day. Sleep keeps you healthy, too!

BRING ON THE ZZZ'S

What causes sleep? Your brain. At bedtime, your brain releases a chemical called melatonin that makes you feel sleepy. Your brain also tells your muscles to relax.

BRAIN BOOST

Sleep helps you concentrate, learn new things, and make good decisions.

MEMORY MAKER

While you sleep, your brain is busy! It sorts through information from your day and stores it as memories.

GROWING UP

You might not feel much taller each morning, but when you sleep, your brain releases a chemical that helps you grow.

DID YOU KNOW?

Horses, elephants, and flamingoes can all sleep standing up.

TELL ME ABOUT IT!

People use words to tell each other how we feel, what we like and don't like, and all sorts of other things. Here's how we communicate those words—and more.

VOICE

When you speak or sing, your lungs push air through flaps in your throat called vocal cords. The cords vibrate, creating sound waves that come out through your mouth. That's your voice!

TONGUE

VOCAL CORDS

If you put your **hand** on your **throat** while you are talking, you can **feel** your **vocal cords** vibrating.

SPEECH

Your vocal cords open and close to change the sounds you make. As those sounds come through your mouth, your tongue, lips, and jaws move to shape the sounds into words.

SINGING

Your vocal folds can move to change the way air is pushed out of your lungs. This adjusts the pitch and volume of your voice to create music.

LANGUAGE

Babies learn to speak the same language—or languages—that the people around them speak. You can also learn languages by visiting new places or taking classes.

I've got a lot to say!

WRITING

In many languages, writing is made up of letters that represent the sounds in a word. In some languages, written symbols represent things or ideas.

Sign Language

Many people who are deaf or cannot hear well use this special language. They communicate by moving their hands and using facial expressions. Even if you don't know sign language, you use your hands and face to communicate. Try using your hands to say "Hello" or "Come here." How can your face show someone that you're happy? Sad? Surprised?

THIS SIGN MEANS "THANK YOU" IN AMERICAN SIGN LANGUAGE.

THAT'S COOL!

SEE YOUR BODY UP CLOSE!

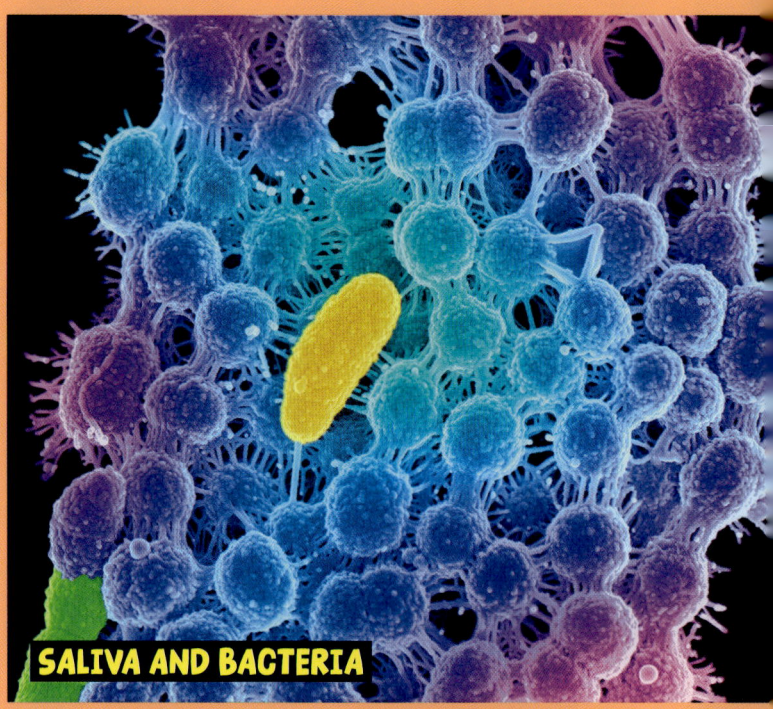

SALIVA AND BACTERIA

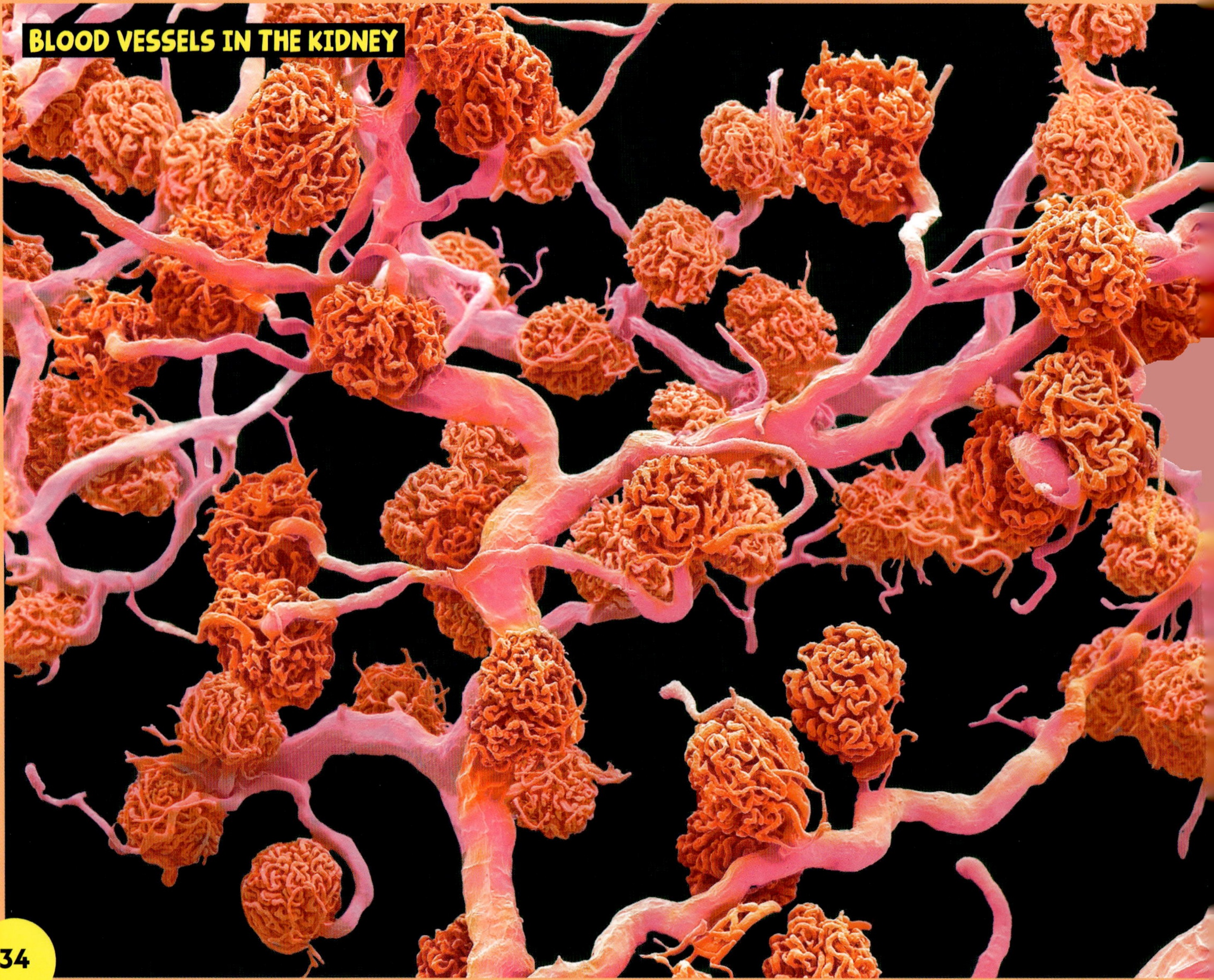

BLOOD VESSELS IN THE KIDNEY

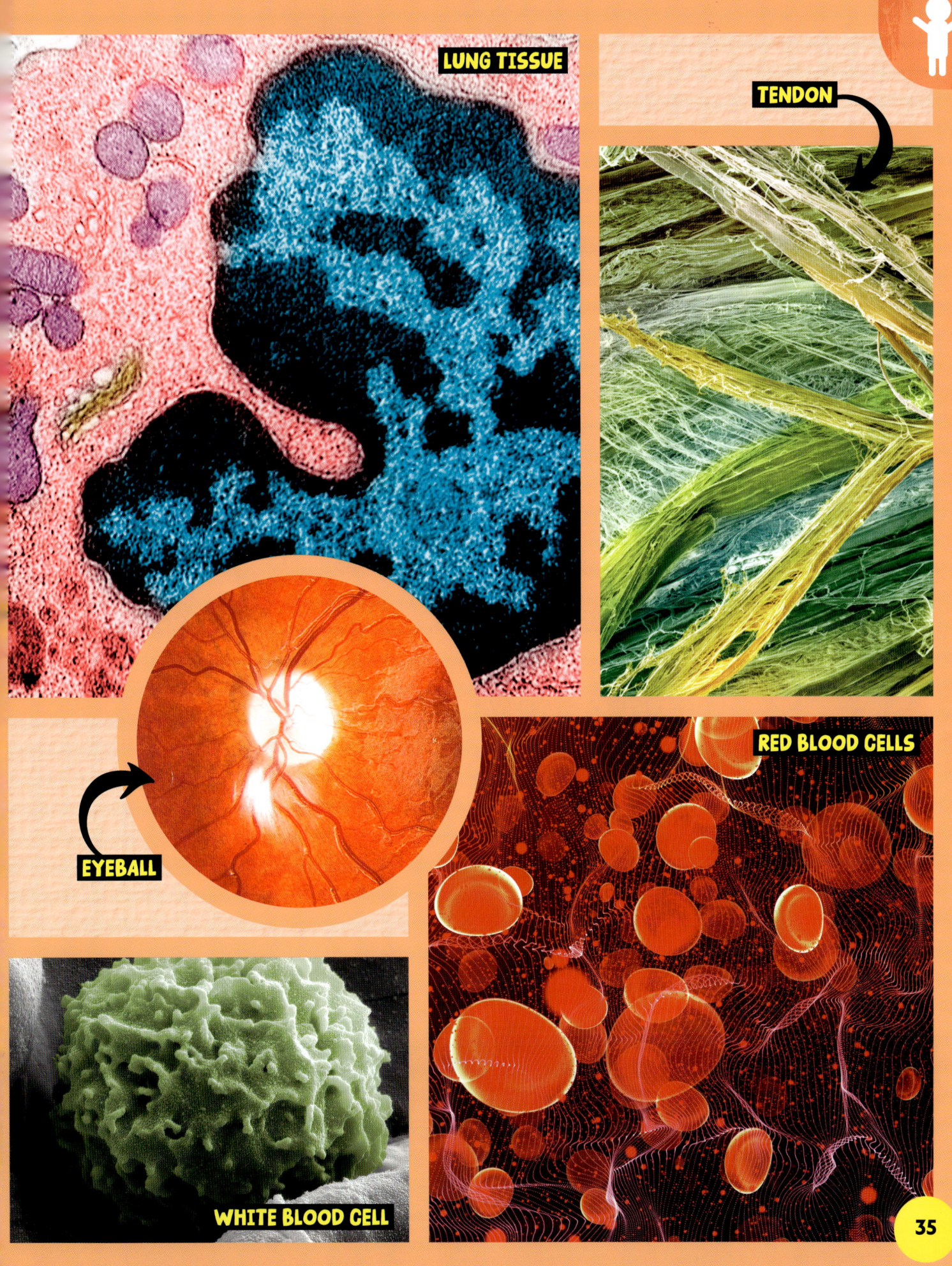

LUNG TISSUE

TENDON

EYEBALL

RED BLOOD CELLS

WHITE BLOOD CELL

35

CHAPTER 2

Down to Earth

Earth is covered with **forests, mountains, deserts,** and lots of **water.** It is filled with **plants** and **animals**—including you! This chapter takes a peek into our **HOME PLANET.**

The word "earth" can also mean soil or the ground.

HOME SWEET EARTH

We live on a beautiful planet called Earth. From space it looks mostly blue, because so much of it is covered by oceans. The rest of Earth's surface is land.

Earth **spins around** and around at **1,000 miles** an hour (1,600 km/h)!

DID YOU KNOW?

Earth **moves** around the sun in a **path** called an **orbit**. It takes **one year** for Earth to make **one trip** all the way around **the sun.**

Night and Day

Earth spins all the way around, or rotates, one time every 24 hours. That equals one entire day and night.

DAY

When the place we live faces the sun, it's time to wake up!

NIGHT

When the place we live faces away from the sun, say good night!

EARTH'S LAYERS

Earth is made up of four different layers. You're standing on one of them right now! The other three layers are too hot and too deep for people to reach.

Earth is 4.5 billion years old.

CRUST

The crust is Earth's outer layer. It is made of many kinds of solid rock. All life on Earth lives here.

MANTLE

Earth's mantle is mostly solid rock. This thick layer makes up most of our planet.

OUTER CORE

This layer of Earth is made of metals like iron and nickel. The outer core is so hot that the metals are liquid!

INNER CORE

The center of Earth is solid. It is also made of metals.

39

MOVING AND SHAKING

It might seem like you are standing on a rock-solid planet. But Earth's surface is made up of moving pieces!

PACIFIC PLATE

JUAN DE FUCA PLATE

NORTH AMERICAN PLATE

COCOS PLATE

CARIBBEAN PLATE

NASCA PLATE

SOUTH AMERICAN PLATE

SCOTIA PLATE

EURASIAN PLATE

AFRICAN PLATE (Nubian)

ARABIAN PLATE

AFRICAN PLATE (Somalian)

INDIAN PLATE

PHILIPPINE PLATE

PACIFIC PLATE

AUSTRALIAN PLATE

ANTARCTIC PLATE

TECTONIC PLATES

Earth's surface, or crust, is made up of giant slabs of rock that fit together like a jigsaw puzzle. These slabs are called tectonic plates.

The **Pacific plate** is the **largest tectonic plate** on Earth's crust.

FAULT LINES

The edges where tectonic plates touch are called fault lines. When the plates pull apart, slide past each other, or crash together, they cause part of Earth's surface to rumble and shake. It's an earthquake!

PULL APART

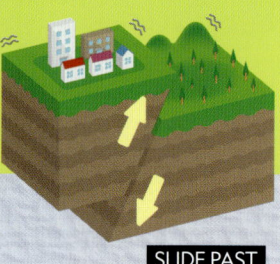

SLIDE PAST

CRASH

CHAIN REACTION

An earthquake can cause other shifts on Earth's surface. Quakes that happen on the ocean floor might trigger a tsunami—a type of giant wave that can travel fast onto land.

Sizing It Up

When there's an earthquake in one place, the vibrations, or waves, travel through the whole planet. Scientists use instruments called seismometers to record the speed and strength of these waves. The wiggly lines on the readout from the seismometer represent the vibrations of an earthquake.

READOUT FROM A SEISMOMETER

Earthquakes can sometimes cause a lot of **damage** to roads and **buildings.**

MAKING MOUNTAINS

When tectonic plates crash together, they can also push Earth's surface upward. Over millions of years, mountains are made!

ERUPTION!

Deep inside our planet it is super hot. The heat melts rocks into a liquid. Sometimes the liquid rock comes out through an opening in Earth's surface. A volcano has erupted!

GASES AND ASH

When a volcano erupts, hot gases, ash, and dust can shoot into the air.

LAVA

When magma flows out of a volcano, it is called lava. It flows over the land.

ROCK

When lava cools, it hardens into solid rock. Each eruption spreads more lava and makes the volcano bigger.

VENT

Magma bubbles or bursts through this opening in Earth's crust.

CONDUIT

The conduit is like a pipe. Magma travels through it to reach Earth's surface.

MAGMA

Fiery hot melted rock called magma pushes up from deep inside Earth.

FOUR TYPES OF VOLCANOES

CINDER CONE VOLCANO ▶

These volcanoes form when exploding lava hardens into ashes and tiny pieces of rock, or cinders. They create a steep cone-shaped hill.

◀ COMPOSITE VOLCANO

These large volcanoes form when multiple explosions of lava, ash, and cinder occur over time.

SHIELD VOLCANO ▶

Eruptions from shield volcanoes, like this one, often have runny lava that flows in all directions.

◀ LAVA DOME VOLCANO

These volcanoes form when the lava is too thick to flow very far. It piles up around the volcano's vent, or opening.

EARTH ROCKS

Rocks are everywhere. They can be small like pebbles or big like mountains. There are three main kinds of rocks. Each one is formed in a different way.

IGNEOUS ROCKS

Igneous rocks form when melted rock, or magma, cools and hardens. Most of Earth's surface is made of igneous rock.

PINK GRANITE

Devil's Tower in Wyoming, U.S.A., is made of **igneous rock.**

SEDIMENTARY ROCKS

These rocks form when layers of sand, mud, and bits of other rocks settle. Over time the layers stick together and form sedimentary rocks.

LIMESTONE

SEDIMENTARY ROCK FORMATION

METAMORPHIC ROCKS

As Earth's tectonic plates move, some rocks get buried, squished, and heated until they change into a whole new rock. These new rocks are called metamorphic rocks.

MARBLE

METAMORPHIC ROCKS ON A BEACH

THE ROCK CYCLE

Rocks are always changing. For example, wind and water break rocks into smaller pieces. It can take millions of years for one type of rock to change into another type. Scientists call this process the rock cycle.

A scientist who **studies rocks** is called a **geologist.**

IGNEOUS ROCKS

Magma breaks through the surface. It cools into igneous rock.

MAGMA

Deep inside Earth, heat and pressure can melt rocks into magma. Then the cycle starts over again.

VOLCANIC ERUPTION

SEDIMENT

Rocks break down into small bits called sediment.

SEDIMENTARY ROCKS

Sediment sticks together to make new rocks.

METAMORPHIC ROCKS

Rocks get heated and squeezed, and the minerals change.

ROCK STARS

A rock you see at the park could have come from inside a volcano, or maybe even from the ocean. Here are a few of the rocks found on Earth.

SANDSTONE

This sedimentary rock is made of bits of sand from either a beach or a desert.

PUMICE

Most rocks sink in water. Not this one! A powerful volcanic eruption can make lava fill up with gas bubbles. The igneous rock that forms from this cooled lava is filled with holes.

GRANITE

This igneous rock is one of the hardest rocks in the world. It can be used to make big buildings or kitchen countertops.

Most **metamorphic rocks** form deep **inside Earth.** Over time they are **pushed up** to the **surface**, where we can **see** them.

COAL

This sedimentary rock is formed from a living thing! Coal is made from dead plants that have hardened over time.

MARBLE

Heat and pressure underground change limestone into this glossy metamorphic rock.

LIMESTONE

One type of this sedimentary rock is made of tiny pieces of seashells.

BASALT

This dark gray igneous rock forms when lava quickly cools on Earth's surface.

SLATE

This metamorphic rock is used for roof and floor tiles. Slate forms in layers.

DID YOU KNOW?

Gymnasts use powdered chalk, a type of limestone, to keep their hands from slipping off bars.

RED CORUNDUM (RUBY)

GOLD

MAGICAL MINERALS

Most rocks are made of minerals. Minerals can be different shapes, colors, and sizes. What color is each of the minerals you see here?

QUARTZ

LABRADORITE

Each **mineral** forms in its own **special shape**, called a **crystal**.

AQUAMARINE

TURQUOISE

DIAMOND

FLUORITE

PURPLE QUARTZ (AMETHYST)

SULFUR

MALACHITE

BLUE CORUNDUM (SAPPHIRE)

SURFACE SIGHTS

From freezing glaciers to winding rivers, the surface of our planet is full of amazing sights and shapes.

GLACIER

Glaciers form in cold areas where a lot of snow falls in one place. Over many years, the snow builds up and becomes thick fields of ice.

WATERFALL

A waterfall is part of a river or stream where the water plunges over a rocky ledge or cliff.

MOUNTAIN

This landform rises high above the ground. It usually has steep slopes and a rounded or pointy peak. A long chain or group of mountains is called a range.

PLATEAU

A plateau is a flat landform that rises high above the surrounding area.

PRAIRIE

Prairies are huge areas of flat grassland with few trees.

RIVER

A river is a large stream of moving fresh water. A river starts in one location and flows into a lake or an ocean.

CANYON

This landform is a deep valley between steep cliffs. A canyon can be narrow or wide.

A river's flowing water slowly **wears away** rocks to create a canyon. It can take **millions** of years for a **canyon** to **form.**

VALLEY

A valley is a low area of land surrounded by higher areas of land, like hills or mountains.

BIOMES

Biomes are areas of Earth that have similar plants and animals. Here are six types of biomes, or major life zones.

FOREST

Forests are large areas of land covered with many trees, shrubs, and other plants. Forests grow in almost every part of the planet. They are home to many different kinds of animals.

MARINE

Saltwater oceans cover most of our planet's surface. Millions of plants and animals live in Earth's largest biome. Estuaries, where rivers and streams meet the oceans, are also part of this biome.

FRESH WATER

Fresh water can be found in ponds, lakes, streams, rivers, and wetlands across the globe. Unlike ocean water, fresh water is not salty.

DESERT

Deserts are the driest places on Earth. The plants and animals that live in deserts can survive without much water.

TUNDRA

Brr! This is the coldest of all the biomes. The land is frozen for between six and 10 months of the year.

GRASSLAND

Grasses cover these large and open areas of land. Not enough rain falls for tall trees to grow. Grasslands get more rain than deserts but less than forests.

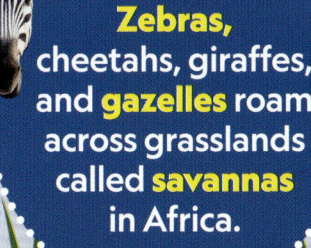

Zebras, cheetahs, giraffes, and **gazelles** roam across grasslands called **savannas** in Africa.

WATER CYCLE

Water travels from oceans, lakes, and rivers to the air and then back down again. This journey is called the water cycle.

2. CONDENSATION

The water vapor rises higher into the air. It cools and turns back into liquid water. The water droplets stick together to form rain. Or they might freeze to form ice crystals.

1. EVAPORATION

The sun heats water, which turns the liquid water into a gas called water vapor.

The **rain** that **falls** today is the **same water** that fell on the **dinosaurs!**

Liquid, Solid, or Gas?

Everything on Earth is made of matter, from the book you're holding to the grass you walk on. Matter exists in one of three forms, or states: solid, liquid, and gas. On Earth, water can be found in all three forms. When the sun heats liquid water on Earth's surface, it becomes water vapor, or gas, that rises up to the skies. Ice, the solid form of water, can be found in snow or hail.

LIQUID SOLID

GAS

3. PRECIPITATION

The water droplets and ice crystals get larger and heavier. Then they fall from the clouds as rain or snow.

4. RUNOFF

Rain, snow, and melting ice fill Earth's oceans, lakes, and rivers with water.

COOL CLOUDS

Clouds come in many different sizes and shapes. No matter what they look like, all clouds are made of the same thing: water floating in the sky.

CIRRUS

These thin, wispy clouds high in the sky are made of ice crystals.

CUMULUS

These fluffy white clouds have flat bottoms and round tops.

Have you ever seen animal-shaped clouds?

Heavy as a Cloud

Clouds look light. But tiny water droplets in the clouds make them heavy. A fluffy cumulus cloud weighs more than one million pounds (454,000 kg). That's as much as about 70 African elephants!

LENTICULAR

Is that an alien spaceship or a cloud? It's a cloud that often forms near mountains.

Fog is a cloud you can **walk through.** It hangs low over **land** or **water.**

STRATUS

These flat gray clouds stretch across the sky. Sometimes they even touch the ground and become fog.

MAMMATUS

These clouds look like a bunch of pouches hanging from the sky. They usually form under storm clouds.

CUMULONIMBUS

These enormous clouds are also called thunderheads. They can bring storms with rain, wind, thunder, and lightning.

WILD WEATHER

Weather describes what it is like outside every day. Is it cloudy? Sunny? Snowing? Raining? Weather can change all the time. What kind of weather do you have today?

SNOW

Snow falls when it is cold enough for water droplets in the clouds to freeze. The droplets turn into tiny ice crystals called snowflakes.

No two **snowflakes** are exactly the **same!**

SUN

The sun warms our planet. On a clear day, the sunlight is bright and hot. You can feel the warm sun on your skin.

RAIN

Rain is water falling from the sky. It comes from clouds. Clouds are filled with water droplets. These water droplets bump into each other and form bigger droplets. When the droplets get too heavy, they fall to Earth.

WIND

Wind is moving air. You can hear and feel wind. You can see it gently carry the fluff of a dandelion. But sometimes wind is so powerful that it can push over a tree.

DID YOU KNOW?

Sunlight and trillions of tiny raindrops in the air combine to create a rainbow in the sky.

STORM ALERT

Sometimes the weather on Earth is wild!
Check out some of these extreme events.

TORNADO

A thunderstorm can create a column of fast-spinning air called a tornado. A tornado is strong enough to rip a house apart or toss a car into the air.

THUNDERSTORM

If you hear thunder and see a flash of lightning during a downpour of rain, that is a thunderstorm. You might see little balls of ice, or hail, fall to the ground, too.

CYCLONE

A tropical cyclone, or hurricane, is a giant spinning storm that starts over warm ocean waters. If it comes onto land, it causes flooding, tornadoes, and wind damage.

FLOOD

A flood happens when a lot of rain, melting snow, or giant ocean waves wash over the land. The ground cannot soak up the water fast enough. And if storm drains are blocked, the water has nowhere else to go.

BLIZZARD

Snow and strong winds create a blizzard. The blowing snow during this dangerous storm makes it hard to see very far.

SEASONS

The weather where we live usually changes throughout the year. These changes are called seasons: winter, spring, summer, and fall. But what's the reason for these four seasons?

NORTH POLE **AXIS**

EQUATOR

SOUTH POLE

ON AN AXIS

Imagine a stick running through the center of Earth, with one end sticking out the top and the other out the bottom. Earth spins, or rotates, on this imaginary stick called an axis. Now picture the axis tilted to the side. This is the position of Earth as it orbits the sun.

Places near **the poles,** at the **top** and **bottom** of Earth, stay **cold all year.**

CHANGING SEASONS

Earth's tilted axis means that during its year-long trip around the sun, different parts of the planet's surface are tilted toward the sun.

SUN

SUMMER

It's summer in the part of the world tilted toward the sun.

WINTER

It's winter in the part of the world tilted away from the sun.

Places near the Equator, around the middle of Earth, stay **warm** all year.

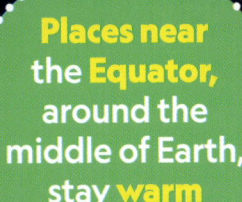

SPRING

In spring, the weather warms. New seedlings sprout, flowers bloom, and trees grow new green leaves.

SUMMER

It gets even warmer outside in summer. Splash! You can take a dip to cool off under the hot sun.

FALL

In fall, it gets cooler. Leaves on the trees start to turn red, orange, and yellow.

WINTER

The weather gets colder in winter. Snow might fall where you live!

Celebrating Seasons

On February 2 in the United States and Canada, people watch a groundhog come out of his burrow. According to legend, if the groundhog sees his shadow, winter will last for six more weeks. If he doesn't, an early spring is on its way.

THAT'S COOL!

NATURAL WONDERS

LARGEST WATERFALL:
VICTORIA FALLS, BORDER OF ZAMBIA AND ZIMBABWE

LARGEST CAVE:
SON DOONG, VIETNAM

DEEPEST CANYON:
YARLUNG TSANGPO
GRAND CANYON, CHINA

LIMESTONE TERRACES:
PAMUKKALE, TURKEY

EYE-POPPING PINK:
LAKE HILLIER, AUSTRALIA

RAINBOW MOUNTAINS:
GANSU, CHINA

TALLEST MOUNTAIN:
MOUNT EVEREST,
BORDER OF TIBET
AND NEPAL

CHAPTER 3

Big Wide World

Do you like to **explore?** Discover **new places?** Track down the home of your **FAVORITE ANIMAL?** The world is full of **incredible** and **exciting things.** A map will help you **FIND IT ALL.**

People have been making maps for thousands of years.

SEE THE WORLD— ON A MAP!

People use maps to explore places that are nearby and places that are far away. Maps can show you where to find cities, countries, oceans, and more. A map can also help you find where you are and where you want to go.

COMPASS ROSE

A map's compass rose shows directions: North, South, East, and West.

N

W   E

S

W

W FOR WEST

West is the direction where the sun sets at night.

MAP KEY

A map key tells you what the lines, colors, and symbols on the map mean.

NORTH AMERICA

ATLANTIC OCEAN

PACIFIC OCEAN

Equator

SOUTH AMERICA

MAP KEY

- Africa
- Antarctica
- Asia
- Australia, New Zealand, and Oceania
- Europe
- North America
- South America
- Ocean
- Equator

N FOR NORTH

North points toward the North Pole, the northernmost part of Earth.

N

DID YOU KNOW?

Continents are large areas of land on Earth. There are seven: North America, South America, Europe, Asia, Africa, Australia, and Antarctica.

ARCTIC OCEAN

EQUATOR

The Equator is an imaginary line that wraps around the center of Earth. It is halfway between the North Pole and the South Pole.

EUROPE

ASIA

E FOR EAST

East is the direction where the sun rises in the morning.

AFRICA

PACIFIC OCEAN

Equator

E ▶

INDIAN OCEAN

AUSTRALIA, NEW ZEALAND, AND OCEANIA

DID YOU KNOW?

A person who makes maps is called a cartographer.

SOUTHERN OCEAN

ANTARCTICA

S FOR SOUTH

South points toward the South Pole, the southernmost part of Earth.

S

PHYSICAL MAPS

Physical maps, like this one, show mountains, deserts, and other landscape features found on Earth. A physical map can also show streets, parks, and buildings.

N

W E

S

PACIFIC OCEAN

GREENLAND

NORTH AMERICA

ROCKY MOUNTAINS

Mississippi

APPALACHIAN MTS.

WEST INDIES

ATLANTIC OCEAN

ALPS

ATLAS MTS.

S A H A

AFRICA

Equator

The **Pacific Ocean** is the **largest** and **deepest** of Earth's oceans.

ANDES

Amazon

SOUTH AMERICA

ANDES

MAP KEY

- Mountains
- Desert
- Forest
- Grassland
- Wetland
- Tundra
- Ice sheet

SOUTHERN OCEAN

MAP KEY

This map key uses different colors and symbols to show Earth's many landscape features, from ice sheets to wetlands.

The Arctic Ocean is the smallest and shallowest of Earth's oceans.

ARCTIC OCEAN

EUROPE

URAL MTS.

Volga

ASIA

R A

Nile

HIMALAYA

Yangtze

PACIFIC OCEAN

DID YOU KNOW?

A globe is a round mini model of Earth. You have to turn it to see the other side. But a map is flat, which allows you to see the whole Earth at one time.

Equator

INDIAN OCEAN

An island is a body of land surrounded by water. Australia is both a continent and a country!

AUSTRALIA, NEW ZEALAND, AND OCEANIA

MOUNTAINS

A series of mountains is called a range or a chain. Can you spot some on this map?

ANTARCTICA

OCEANS

The continents separate Earth's one big ocean into five parts: the Pacific, Atlantic, Indian, Arctic, and Southern Oceans.

NORTH AMERICA

North America reaches from the island of Greenland in the north to the country of Panama in the south. Forests, deserts, islands, mountains, and rivers create many different kinds of habitats for people and animals.

Alaska (part of the United States)

YELLOWSTONE NATIONAL PARK

Yellowstone National Park in Wyoming, Montana, and Idaho, U.S.A., is the world's first national park. Wolves, American bison, and many other kinds of animals live here.

GRAND PRISMATIC HOT SPRING

AMERICAN BISON

CANADA

PARK

GRAY WOLF

HOMES ON HIGH

Ancestral Puebloans built homes in cliffs in what is now the southwestern United States.

A WARM WINTER HOME

Millions of monarch butterflies flutter through the sky as they migrate from Canada and the United States to spend the winter in mountain forests in Mexico.

MEXICO

MONARCH BUTTERFLIES

POLAR BEARS

Most polar bears live above the Arctic Circle. Thick layers of fur and fat keep these large animals warm.

Greenland
(part of Denmark)

GREAT LAKES

Thousands of years ago, melting glaciers created these enormous freshwater lakes.

DID YOU KNOW?

The Great Lakes are so big that they have waves like the ocean.

FLORIDA MANATEE

SUPER SWAMP

The Everglades in Florida, U.S.A., is a huge wetland. It is home to all kinds of wildlife, including alligators, panthers, manatees, and many kinds of birds.

AMERICAN ALLIGATOR

UNITED STATES

THE BAHAMAS

DOMINICAN REPUBLIC

ST. KITTS & NEVIS

ANTIGUA & BARBUDA

BELIZE

CUBA

DOMINICA

GUATEMALA

JAMAICA

HAITI

ST. LUCIA

HONDURAS

BARBADOS

ST. VINCENT & THE GRENADINES

NICARAGUA

EL SALVADOR

GRENADA

TRINIDAD & TOBAGO

COSTA RICA

PANAMA

ARCTIC OCEAN

NORTH AMERICA

EUROPE

ASIA

ATLANTIC OCEAN

AFRICA

PACIFIC OCEAN

PACIFIC OCEAN

SOUTH AMERICA

INDIAN OCEAN

AUSTRALIA, NEW ZEALAND, AND OCEANIA

SOUTHERN OCEAN

ANTARCTICA

SOUTH AMERICA

South America stretches from the Caribbean Sea to the icy cold waters of the Southern Ocean. This continent is home to the world's biggest rainforest and the tall Andes Mountains.

GALÁPAGOS ISLANDS

GALÁPAGOS FUR SEAL

These 19 islands off the coast of South America are home to giant tortoises, marine iguanas, and Galápagos fur seals.

Galápagos Islands
(part of Ecuador)

Volcanoes formed the **Galápagos** Islands.

ANDEAN CLOUD FORESTS

Cloud forests get their name from the low clouds that cover the mountains.

MACHU PICCHU

You can still walk on the ruins of this city in the Andes Mountains that the Inca people built thousands of years ago.

VENEZUELA

COLOMBIA

ECUADOR

PERU

ANDES

BOLIVIA

ANDES

ARGENTINA

CHILE

AMAZON RAINFOREST

This huge rainforest covers nearly half of South America. From monkeys and macaws to poison frogs and jaguars, many kinds of animals live here.

BLUE-AND-YELLOW MACAWS

GUYANA

SURINAME

French Guiana (part of France)

Amazon

BRAZIL

PARAGUAY

SQUIRREL MONKEYS

AMAZON RIVER

The Amazon carries more water than any other river in the world. The longest stretch of the river flows through Brazil.

CAPYBARAS

Meet the biggest relative of the guinea pig! Capybaras can hide in the water to escape the hungry jaguars and anacondas that want to eat them.

SÃO PAULO, BRAZIL

This is the largest city in South America.

URUGUAY

Falkland Islands (part of the United Kingdom)

ARCTIC OCEAN

NORTH AMERICA

EUROPE

ASIA

ATLANTIC OCEAN

AFRICA

PACIFIC OCEAN

PACIFIC OCEAN

SOUTH AMERICA

INDIAN OCEAN

AUSTRALIA, NEW ZEALAND, AND OCEANIA

SOUTHERN OCEAN

ANTARCTICA

EUROPE

Europe is the second smallest continent, but it has a lot of countries! Several of its big cities are on the coasts or along its many long rivers.

PEDAL POWER

In Copenhagen, Denmark, people pedal their bikes to work and school across the capital city's bridges and bike paths.

ICELAND

STONEHENGE

People built these circles of gigantic stones thousands of years ago in what is now England. England, Wales, Scotland, and Northern Ireland make up the United Kingdom.

SWEDEN

NORWAY

UNITED KINGDOM

LATVIA

IRELAND

DENMARK

Part of Russia

1

2

3

GERMANY

POLAND

THE MATTERHORN

The Matterhorn, rising high in the Alps mountain range, is shaped like a pyramid. Each of its four sides faces a different direction: east, west, north, and south.

SWITZERLAND

FRANCE

4

CZECHIA

AUSTRIA

SLOVAKIA

HUNGARY

9

CROATIA

PORTUGAL

SPAIN

5

6

7

ITALY

8

10 SERBIA

11 12

13 14

GREECE

ROMAN COLOSSEUM

This giant theater in Rome, Italy, was built nearly 2,000 years ago. Time and earthquakes have caused much of it to fall down.

MALTA

VENICE, ITALY

People in Venice, Italy, often travel through the city on boats. Its water-filled "streets" are called canals.

THE SAMI PEOPLE

The Sami people live in parts of Norway, Finland, Sweden, and Russia. Reindeer herding is a tradition in Sami culture.

DID YOU KNOW?

At least 80 rivers flow through the city of St. Petersburg, Russia.

1. **NETHERLANDS**
2. **BELGIUM**
3. **LUXEMBOURG**
4. **LIECHTENSTEIN**
5. **ANDORRA**
6. **MONACO**
7. **SAN MARINO**
8. **VATICAN CITY**
9. **SLOVENIA**
10. **BOSNIA & HERZEGOVINA**
11. **MONTENEGRO**
12. **KOSOVO**
13. **ALBANIA**
14. **NORTH MACEDONIA**

FINLAND

ESTONIA

LITHUANIA

BELARUS

RUSSIA

KAZAKHSTAN

UKRAINE

ROMANIA

MOLDOVA

Danube

BULGARIA

TÜRKİYE (TURKEY)

AZERBAIJAN

CYPRUS

MUD VOLCANOES

More than 300 mud volcanoes—which spew mud instead of lava—are found in the small country of Azerbaijan.

LONG RIVER

The Danube River runs through nine countries. It is a source of fresh drinking water for millions of people.

ARCTIC OCEAN

NORTH AMERICA

EUROPE

ASIA

ATLANTIC OCEAN

AFRICA

PACIFIC OCEAN

PACIFIC OCEAN

SOUTH AMERICA

INDIAN OCEAN

AUSTRALIA, NEW ZEALAND, AND OCEANIA

SOUTHERN OCEAN

ANTARCTICA

AFRICA

Half of Africa is above the Equator and includes the world's largest hot desert, the Sahara. The other half of the continent is below the Equator and includes grasslands and tropical rainforests.

MOROCCO

Marrakech, Morocco, is called the Red City for the color of its buildings.

Western Sahara
(claimed by Morocco)

MOROCCO

TUNISIA

ALGERIA

LIBYA

S A H A R A

CABO VERDE

MAURITANIA

MALI

NIGER

CHAD

SENEGAL

THE GAMBIA

GUINEA-BISSAU

GUINEA

BURKINA FASO

BENIN

NIGERIA

SIERRA LEONE

CÔTE D'IVOIRE

TOGO

LIBERIA

GHANA

CAMEROON

EQUATORIAL GUINEA

GABON

Equator

SAO TOME AND PRINCIPE

CONGO

ANGOLA

NAMIBIA

SERENGETI PLAINS

Lions, giraffes, zebras, wild dogs, African elephants, and wildebeests roam the tall grass savanna of Africa's Serengeti. Savannas are found near the Equator where it is warm all year.

AFRICAN ELEPHANT

AFRICAN LION

VICTORIA FALLS

This is the world's tallest waterfall. The mist from the falling water can be seen from miles away.

EGYPTIAN PYRAMIDS

Thousands of years ago, ancient Egyptians built pyramids as tombs for their rulers, called pharaohs.

People have **lived** in Africa longer than any **other place.** Scientists think that **humans** came from here.

NILE RIVER

The Nile River, Africa's longest, flows through 11 countries.

FOSSA

MADAGASCAR

This island off the coast of Africa is home to animals found nowhere else on Earth, such as lemurs, aye-ayes, fossae, and some chameleons.

PANTHER CHAMELEON

EGYPT

A

Nile

SUDAN

ERITREA

DJIBOUTI

CENTRAL AFRICAN REPUBLIC

SOUTH SUDAN

ETHIOPIA

DEMOCRATIC REPUBLIC OF THE CONGO

UGANDA

KENYA

SOMALIA

RWANDA

BURUNDI

TANZANIA

SEYCHELLES

MALAWI

COMOROS

ZAMBIA

ZIMBABWE

MOZAMBIQUE

MAURITIUS

MADAGASCAR

BOTSWANA

ESWATINI (SWAZILAND)

SOUTH AFRICA

LESOTHO

ARCTIC OCEAN

NORTH AMERICA

EUROPE

ASIA

ATLANTIC OCEAN

PACIFIC OCEAN

AFRICA

PACIFIC OCEAN

SOUTH AMERICA

INDIAN OCEAN

AUSTRALIA, NEW ZEALAND, AND OCEANIA

SOUTHERN OCEAN

ANTARCTICA

MOUNT KILIMANJARO

Africa's tallest mountain, Mount Kilimanjaro in Tanzania, is a volcano.

ASIA

Asia is Earth's largest continent. It covers almost one-third of our planet! More people live in Asia than on all the other continents combined.

CAPPADOCIA

Soar above the rock pillars—nicknamed fairy chimneys—that rise high above the valleys in Cappadocia, Türkiye (Turkey).

DEAD SEA

The water in this lake is much saltier than the ocean. It is so salty that no animals or plants can live in it.

Asia has the **highest** (the Himalaya) and **lowest** (the Dead Sea) places on **Earth's surface.**

RUSSIA
GEORGIA
ARMENIA
LEBANON
ISRAEL
TÜRKİYE (TURKEY)
SYRIA
AZERBAIJAN
KAZAKHSTAN
UZBEKISTAN
IRAQ
EGYPT
JORDAN
KUWAIT
TURKMENISTAN
KYRGYZSTAN
TAJIKISTAN
IRAN
SAUDI ARABIA
QATAR
AFGHANISTAN
NEPAL
BAHRAIN
PAKISTAN
YEMEN
OMAN
UNITED ARAB EMIRATES
INDIA
MALDIVES
SRI LANKA

TAJ MAHAL

It took more than 20 years and 20,000 workers to build this marble tomb for the wife of India's emperor.

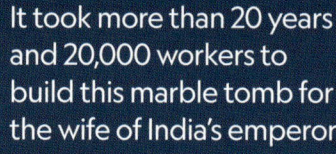

HIMALAYA

This mountain range includes the world's highest mountain, Mount Everest.

BAIKAL SEALS

LAKE BAIKAL

Lake Baikal in Siberia is the deepest lake in the world. The world's only freshwater seal, the nerpa, calls these waters home.

GIANT PANDAS

These black-and-white bears live in bamboo forests in the mountains of China.

COLOSSAL CAVE

Vietnam is home to the world's largest cave. Some parts of Son Doong are so big that a skyscraper could fit inside. A river flows through it, and a rainforest grows there, too!

RICE

Most of the world's rice is grown in Asia, in flooded fields called paddies.

RUSSIA

MONGOLIA

NORTH KOREA

SOUTH KOREA

JAPAN

CHINA

BHUTAN

BANGLADESH

MYANMAR

LAOS

THAILAND

CAMBODIA

VIETNAM

TAIWAN

PHILIPPINES

BRUNEI

MALAYSIA

INDONESIA

SINGAPORE

TIMOR-LESTE

ARCTIC OCEAN

NORTH AMERICA

EUROPE

ASIA

ATLANTIC OCEAN

AFRICA

PACIFIC OCEAN

PACIFIC OCEAN

SOUTH AMERICA

INDIAN OCEAN

AUSTRALIA, NEW ZEALAND, AND OCEANIA

SOUTHERN OCEAN

ANTARCTICA

AUSTRALIA, NEW ZEALAND, AND OCEANIA

This big region includes Australia, the world's smallest continent, as well as New Zealand and Oceania, a group of more than 10,000 islands in the Pacific Ocean.

FEDERATED STATES OF MICRONESIA

MARSHALL ISLANDS

PALAU

NAURU

KIRIBATI

SYDNEY OPERA HOUSE

This concert hall, the city's best known landmark, is heated and air-conditioned using seawater from Sydney Harbor.

PAPUA NEW GUINEA

SOLOMON ISLANDS

VANUATU

TUVALU

FIJI

New Caledonia (part of France)

AUSTRALIA

ULURU

Uluru in Australia is one huge rock! It takes about four hours to walk all the way around it.

NEW ZEALAND

Corals look like **plants,** but they are **animals** that form **reefs.**

GREAT BARRIER REEF

Australia is home to the world's largest coral reef, the Great Barrier Reef. Sharks, rays, whales, dolphins, sea turtles, and fish are found here.

KOALAS

GRAY KANGAROO

MARSUPIALS

Kangaroos, koalas, and wombats are only found in the wild in Australia. They are marsupials, a kind of mammal.

Most of the **Fiji islands** were formed by **underwater volcanoes.**

K I R I B A T I

SAMOA

Cook Islands (part of New Zealand)

TONGA

French Polynesia (part of France)

PAPUA NEW GUINEA

More than 800 different languages are spoken in this island country!

LIGHTING THE DARK

Glowworms dangle inside the Waitomo Caves in New Zealand. They glow to attract insects to eat.

KIWIS

Kiwis live in the wild only in New Zealand. This unusual bird cannot fly.

ARCTIC OCEAN
NORTH AMERICA
EUROPE
ASIA
ATLANTIC OCEAN
AFRICA
PACIFIC OCEAN
PACIFIC OCEAN
SOUTH AMERICA
INDIAN OCEAN
AUSTRALIA, NEW ZEALAND, AND OCEANIA
SOUTHERN OCEAN
ANTARCTICA

81

ANTARCTICA

Welcome to Antarctica, the coldest, windiest, and driest continent on Earth! There are many more penguins, seals, and whales than people in this land of ice.

SOUTH POLE

The South Pole, the southernmost part of the world, is in Antarctica.

STUDY SPOT

People do not live in Antarctica year-round. But scientists from around the world visit research stations there to study the continent's climate and animals.

ANTARCTIC PENINSULA

RONNE ICE SHELF

ELLSWORTH LAND

TRANSANTARCTIC MOUNTAINS

WEST ANTARCTICA

MARIE BYRD LAND

ROSS ICE SHELF

It is sometimes **so cold** in Antarctica that if you threw **a bucket of water** into the air, the water would **freeze** before it hit the **ground!**

EMPEROR PENGUIN CHICK

ADÉLIE PENGUINS

PENGUINS

Millions of these birds call this frozen world home. Emperor, king, and Adélie penguins lay their eggs on land and hunt for squid and fish in the sea.

HUMPBACK WHALES

These giant mammals swim through Antarctic waters in the summer.

Antarctica is a **desert**—a cold desert, that is! It **rarely snows** there.

QUEEN MAUD LAND

ENDERBY LAND

Lambert Glacier

ANTARCTICA

EAST ANTARCTICA

WILKES LAND

LAMBERT GLACIER

Thick layers of ice called glaciers cover almost all of Antarctica. In some places, the ice is three miles (4.8 km) thick!

SOUTHERN ELEPHANT SEALS

Animals that live here are built to survive the cold. These seals have fat called blubber that protects them from the harsh, icy winds.

MOUNT EREBUS

Mount Erebus is the world's southernmost active volcano.

North Pole · ARCTIC OCEAN

NORTH AMERICA

EUROPE   ASIA

ATLANTIC OCEAN

AFRICA

PACIFIC OCEAN

PACIFIC OCEAN

SOUTH AMERICA

INDIAN OCEAN

AUSTRALIA, NEW ZEALAND, AND OCEANIA

SOUTHERN OCEAN

South Pole · ANTARCTICA

ALBANIA
(double-headed eagle)

ANDORRA
(cows)

BHUTAN
(dragon)

BOLIVIA
(condor, llama)

DOMINICA
(sisserou parrot)

The **sisserou parrot** is found only on the small **Caribbean island** of Dominica.

FABULOUS FLAGS

Every country has a flag to represent it. Many of these flags feature real or mythical animals that symbolize something special about a country.

MOLDOVA
(eagle and aurochs, an ancient cattle)

ECUADOR
(condor)

EGYPT
(golden eagle)

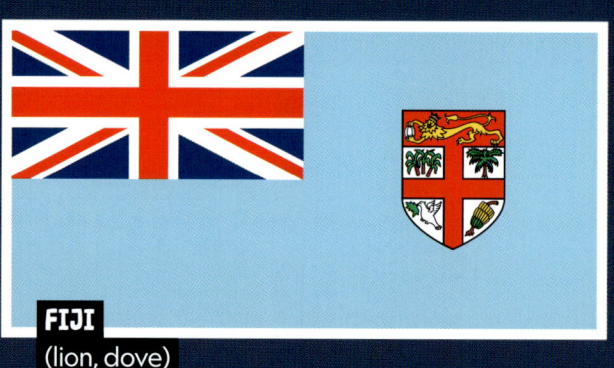

FIJI
(lion, dove)

KAZAKHSTAN
(eagle)

KIRIBATI
(frigate bird)

MEXICO
(eagle, snake)

MONTENEGRO
(double-headed eagle, lion)

PAPUA NEW GUINEA
(bird of paradise)

The vicuña's **thick coat** keeps it **warm** when it's cold in the **Andes Mountains.**

PERU
(vicuña)

SPAIN
(lion)

SRI LANKA
(lion)

GUATEMALA
(quetzal)

UGANDA
(gray crane)

ZAMBIA
(African fish eagle)

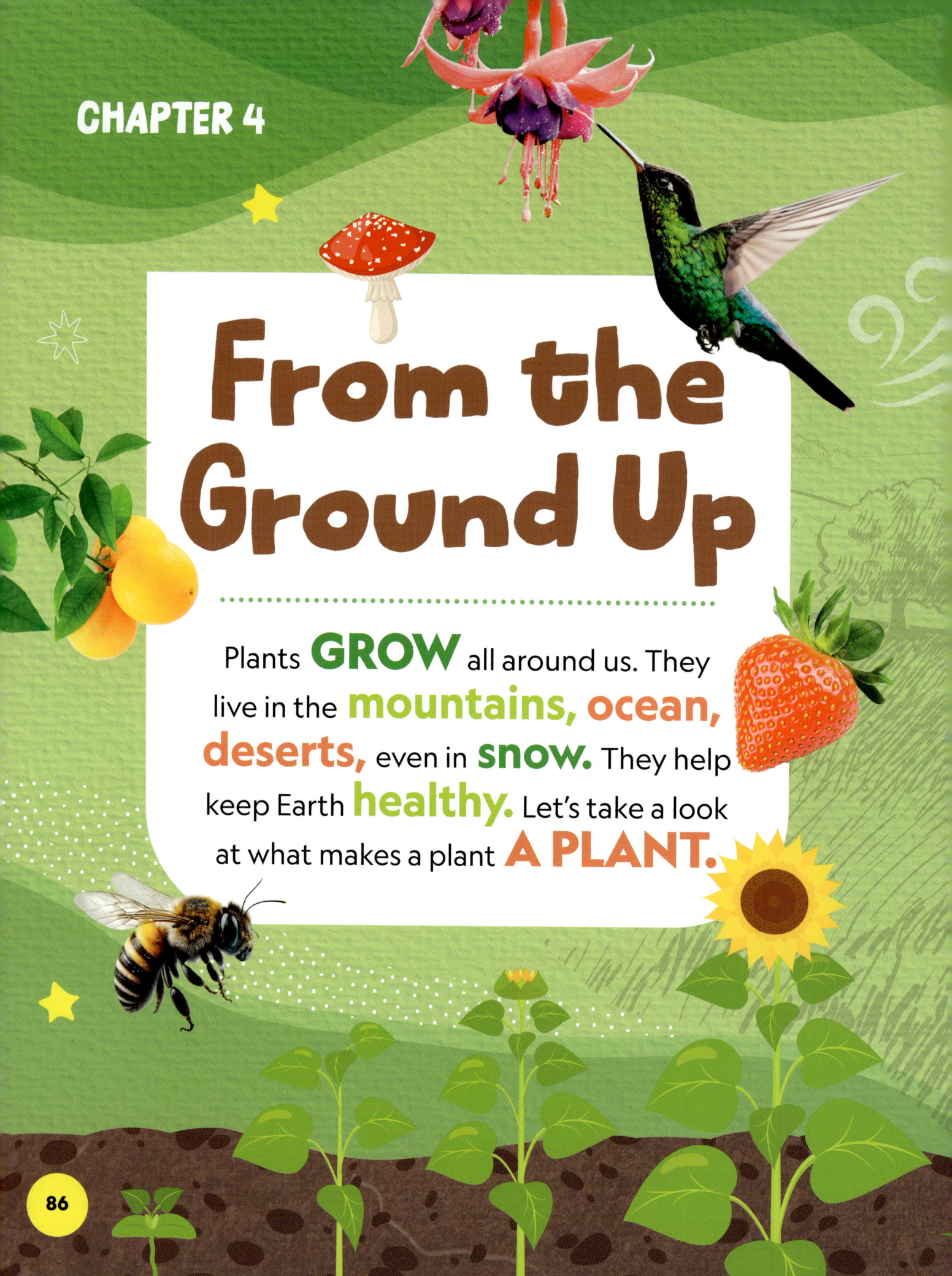

CHAPTER 4

From the Ground Up

Plants **GROW** all around us. They live in the **mountains, ocean, deserts,** even in **snow.** They help keep Earth **healthy.** Let's take a look at what makes a plant **A PLANT.**

WHAT IS A PLANT?

They can't run or hop like animals, but plants are living things, too. They come in all shapes, sizes, and colors. Like all living things, they need water and air to grow. Most plants have roots, stems, and leaves.

LEAVES

Leaves soak up sunlight and a gas called carbon dioxide from the air.

SEEDS

STEMS

Stems carry water and food from the roots to the rest of the plant.

DID YOU KNOW?

One sunflower blossom can make over 1,000 seeds. These seeds make a great snack. Crunch!

Plant Power

Just like you, plants need food to grow. But plants have a superpower: They can make their own food! Sunshine helps a plant's leaves turn air and water into a sugary food. This food flows through the veins in the leaves to the rest of the plant.

FLOWERS

Flowers make seeds so more plants can grow.

Roots can **spread out** or go **down deep** in the soil. This helps them **collect more water.**

ROOTS

Roots hold the plant in the ground. They also work like a straw to pull in water and food from the soil.

HOW PLANTS GROW

Where does a plant come from? Most plants grow from seeds. Let's dig in to find out more. Ready ... set ... sprout!

Seeds need **water to grow,** just like **you.**

PUMPKIN SEED

A pumpkin seed is buried in the dirt. Don't forget to water it!

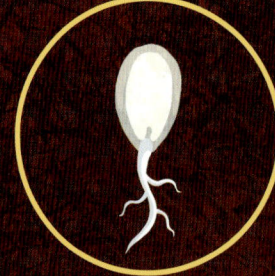

ROOTS

Soon the seed splits. A tiny root peeks out and pokes into the soil.

SPROUT!

A baby pumpkin plant pushes up from the ground. It is called a sprout or a shoot.

A giant **pumpkin** has about **800 seeds.**

LEAVES

The baby plant grows into a leafy vine with yellow flowers.

PUMPKINS

The flowers turn into baby pumpkins. The pumpkins grow bigger and bigger.

MORE SEEDS!

Now a pumpkin is ready to pick. What's inside it? Pumpkin seeds!

Other Ways to Grow

Some plants, like ferns and mosses, don't have flowers and don't grow from seeds. Instead, they grow from tiny things called spores. Mosses have been growing on Earth for millions of years. They can grow in many different places, from cold snowy mountains to hot deserts.

PARTS OF A FLOWER

Bright and beautiful, flowers can make us smile. But flowers have a big job, too. They make seeds! Take a closer look inside this big bloom.

STIGMA
The stigma is the top part of the pistil. It collects the pollen.

PISTIL
The pistil makes the seeds.

ANTHER
The anther is the top part of the stamen.

STAMEN
The stamen makes a sticky powder called pollen.

PETAL
Petals have bright colors and a sweet smell that attract bees and birds.

SEPAL
Sepals protect the flower before it blooms.

NECTARY
The nectary makes nectar, a sweet liquid that attracts bees and birds to the flower.

POLLEN PARTNERS

Pollen sticks to birds, bees, and other animals when they visit a flower. Then the animal carries it to another plant of the same type. This is called pollination. This process helps flowers make seeds to grow new plants.

BAT

Bats visit many kinds of plants.

LIZARD

Pollen sticks to a lizard's scales.

MOTH

Some moths visit flowers at night.

HUMMINGBIRD

Hummingbirds poke their beaks inside flowers.

BUTTERFLY

Butterflies sip nectar from flowers.

BEE

Pollen sticks to a bee's fuzzy body.

The **wind** can also **carry pollen** to other flowers.

93

HOW SEEDS SPREAD

Seeds can be as tiny as a grain of sand or as big as a basketball. They usually have to travel to find their own space to grow in the soil. Here are some ways plants scatter their seeds.

DRIFT

Coconuts fall from palm trees into the sea. These big seeds can float in the water for hundreds or even thousands of miles.

FLOAT

Blow! Dandelion seeds can float a long way on the slightest breeze.

RIDE INSIDE

Birds eat berries in one place, fly away, and then poop out the seeds somewhere else.

FLY

Seeds from a maple tree look like they have wings. They flutter through the air.

STICK

Burrs are seeds covered with prickly spines. They stick to an animal's fur and travel along with it.

POP

When jewelweed seedpods pop open, the seeds shoot out in all directions.

SEED

Seeds to Eat

Some of the foods we eat don't just come from seeds, they *are* seeds! How many of these have you tried?

WALNUTS

PEAS

PEANUTS

POMEGRANATE

One **pomegranate** can hold more than **1,000** seeds.

CASHEWS

LENTILS

PISTACHIOS

CORN

95

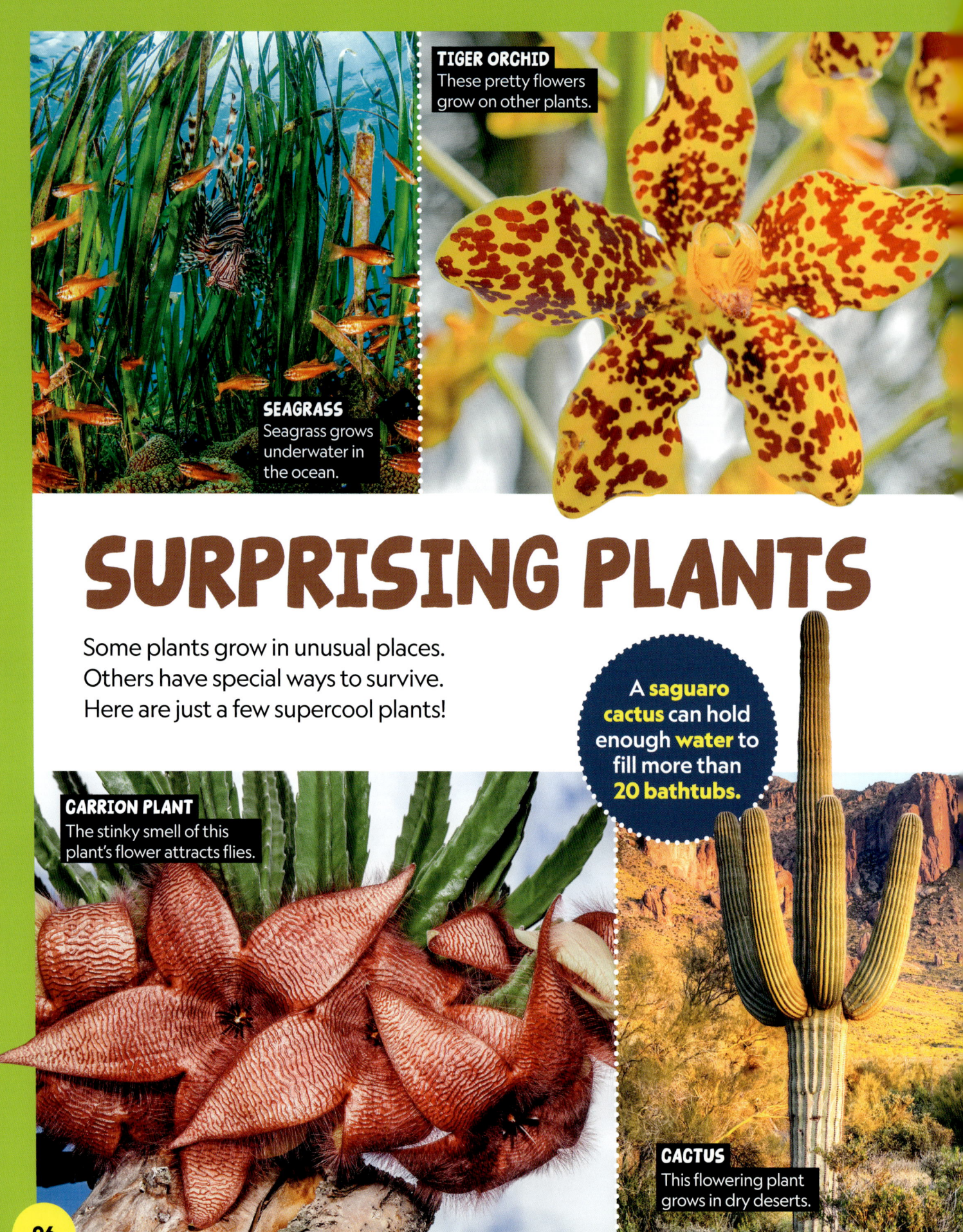

TIGER ORCHID
These pretty flowers grow on other plants.

SEAGRASS
Seagrass grows underwater in the ocean.

SURPRISING PLANTS

Some plants grow in unusual places. Others have special ways to survive. Here are just a few supercool plants!

A **saguaro cactus** can hold enough **water** to fill more than **20 bathtubs.**

CARRION PLANT
The stinky smell of this plant's flower attracts flies.

CACTUS
This flowering plant grows in dry deserts.

LITHOPS
Can you see why these plants are called living stones?

SKELETON FLOWER
You can see through this flower's petals after it rains!

SUCCULENT
These plants grow on hot, dry cliffs. Their leaves can store rainwater.

AMAZONIAN LILY PAD
These lily pads are so large and strong that a small kid can sit on them!

VENUS FLY TRAP
These plants catch bugs with sticky leaves or petals that snap shut.

TERRIFIC TREES

Trees can be tall, short, wide, or curvy. But they all have a woody stem called a trunk, and they all have leaves. Here's how an apple tree changes with the seasons.

Trees that **lose their leaves** in the **fall** are called **deciduous trees.**

APPLE BLOSSOM

SPRING

Rain and warm sunshine help new leaves grow. The leaves use the sun's energy to make food. Flowers bloom next to the new leaves.

SUMMER

The tree is full of green leaves. And look! Fruit is growing on its branches. Soon the apples will be ripe and ready to pick.

FALL

As the weather turns chilly, the tree's leaves stop making food. They change color, from green to yellow to brown. Then they dry up and fall off.

Evergreens

Evergreen trees lose some of their leaves and grow new ones all the time, so they are never bare. They look green all year long. Some evergreens have needle-shaped leaves and make their seeds in cones.

WINTER

The tree's stems and branches are bare. The tree is resting. In the spring it will grow new leaves!

LIFE IN THE TREES

Climb a tree. Read a book in its shade. Trees are a great place to hang out! For an animal, a tree can be even more than a place to play. It's where some animals live, eat, and raise their babies.

Butterflies and ants eat the tree's sugary sap.

Birds build their nest in the tree.

Acorn woodpeckers gather **acorns** and **stash** them in **holes** they **drill** in the branches.

ACORN WOODPECKER

Birds find food in different parts of the tree.

WOOD WARBLER

WOOD MOUSE

DEER

Deer, squirrels, and mice eat the acorns.

Bats roost in loose bark.

One huge **oak tree** can drop **thousands of acorns** in a season.

Moths eat flowers and leaf buds.

Some kinds of owls make their nests in oak trees.

STAG BEETLE

Stag beetles drink sap from the tree.

Pine marten hunt in and around trees.

RED SQUIRREL

Oak trees can live more than 600 years.

FABULOUS FRUIT

Fruits come in all sizes, shapes, and colors. A fruit grows from the flower of a plant. Most fruits have seeds, either on the inside or the outside.

Oranges are grown on **every continent** except **Antarctica.**

DRAGON FRUIT

Inside the scaly skin is a sweet and crunchy fruit!

ORANGES

This bright fruit makes a tasty juice!

STRAWBERRY

The seeds are on the outside of this fruit.

GRAPES

This fruit grows on vines.

PINEAPPLE

The outside may look like a cactus, but this fruit is sweet and juicy inside.

VERY VEGGIE

Vegetables come from the leaves, stems, or roots of a plant. They can grow above the ground, like asparagus and broccoli, or below it, like potatoes, carrots, and onions.

POTATOES

There are more than 5,000 different kinds of potatoes!

WATERMELON RADISH

This bright pink radish is a root you can eat.

CARROTS

Carrots can also be purple, white, and yellow!

KOHLRABI

You can eat both the bulb and the leaves of kohlrabi.

A **tuber** vegetable, such as a potato, is **part** of the plant's **underground stem.**

ROMANESCO BROCCOLI

You're eating bunches of flower buds when you bite into broccoli!

RED ONION

When you cut into an onion, it releases a chemical that can make you cry.

FAR-OUT FUNGI

Fungi are not plants. They do not have roots, stems, leaves, or flowers. But like plants, they are living things. Most fungi grow in shady or dark places. They do not need sunlight to grow.

Mushrooms are fungi. There are thousands of different kinds of mushrooms.

ROSY VEINCAP

Another name for this mushroom is wrinkled peach. Small and rubbery, it grows on stumps and fallen logs.

LION'S MANE

This large shaggy mushroom looks like a white pom-pom, or a lion's mane!

STARFISH FUNGUS

Found on garden mulch or in grassy areas, this fungus grows bright red arms that look like a sea star's.

VEILED LADY

With their delicate white netting, these mushrooms are not hard to find on a tropical forest floor.

VIOLET CORAL FUNGUS

This fungus grows on the ground. Its bright purple stalks are smooth and brittle.

CHICKEN OF THE WOODS

These mushrooms often grow at the base of dead or dying trees.

Some kinds of mushrooms are **poisonous.** You should **never collect** any mushrooms unless an **expert** says they are safe.

CAP

SCALES

RING

STALK

FLY AGARIC

These big mushrooms look like little white eggs when they start to grow on the forest floor. They form bright red caps as they get larger.

FRIENDS OF THE FOREST

What happens when a tree falls on the forest floor? The fungi and creepy-crawlies get to work!

TIMBER!
Mushrooms and other fungi start to grow on the fallen tree.

NEW THREADS
The fungi send tiny hairlike threads into the wood.

WATER BREAK
These threads take in water and nutrients from the tree.

EARTHWORMS

When fungi and animals **break down** a fallen tree, that process is called **decomposition**. It's nature's way of **recycling!**

Most of a **mushroom** grows **underground**. The part we see is called the **fruiting body**.

SPREADING OUT
The fungi spread out. They slowly break down the wood.

BANANA SLUG

SUPER SOIL
Over time, the dead tree is broken down into rich, healthy soil—perfect for new plants to grow in!

A BUGGY FEAST
Beetles, termites, slugs, millipedes, earthworms, and other small creatures eat the rotting wood.

THAT'S COOL!

RECORD BREAKERS

FASTEST-GROWING PLANT:
CHINESE MOSO BAMBOO
CHINA AND TAIWAN

TALLEST TREE:
REDWOODS
CALIFORNIA AND OREGON, U.S.A.

OLDEST TREE:
BRISTLECONE PINES
CALIFORNIA, U.S.A.

BIGGEST FRUIT:
JACKFRUIT
ASIA, AFRICA, AND SOUTH AMERICA

LARGEST FLOWER:
CORPSE FLOWER
INDONESIA

SMALLEST FRUIT:
WATERMEAL
EVERYWHERE EXCEPT ANTARCTICA

BIGGEST SEED:
COCO DE MER
SEYCHELLES

CHAPTER 5

Creature Feature!

We share our planet with all kinds of **ANIMALS.** Some are **big.** Some are **small.** Some **jump.** Some **crawl.** Some **swim** underwater, some **fly** in the sky, some **climb** in trees. They're **EVERYWHERE!**

MARVELOUS MAMMALS

Mammals are the only group of animals that have hair. They drink their mother's milk when they are young, and they use lungs to breathe.

ETRUSCAN SHREW

The Etruscan shrew is one of the smallest mammals on Earth. It uses its long nose to sniff out food.

AFRICAN ELEPHANT

This is the largest mammal on land! An African elephant uses its long trunk to breathe, smell, drink water, pick up food, and even to talk to other elephants.

African elephants flap their big ears to cool off.

BAT

Bats are the only mammals that can fly. They speed through the night sky to find bugs or fruit to eat.

SPIDER MONKEY

This monkey's long arms, legs, and tail help it travel through the trees in its rainforest home.

GRIZZLY BEAR

These huge brown bears have long, strong claws that they use to dig for food and to dig their dens.

Did you know **you** are a **mammal?**

DOLPHIN

Dolphins swim in groups called pods. They make a lot of different sounds to talk to each other. They come to the water's surface to breathe air.

POWERFUL PREDATORS

From tiny weasels to giant orcas, these mammals share something special. They are all predators—animals that hunt and eat other animals.

ERMINE

These small weasels zigzag quickly across the ground to pounce on mice and other small animals.

TIGER

This big cat hunts alone. Its striped coat blends in with leaves and grasses as it waits for prey to pass by. Then it pounces!

Predators are carnivores. They eat meat.

ORCA

These huge dolphins hunt as a team to catch everything from sea turtles to sharks.

POLAR BEAR

These bears are the largest predator on land. They live in the freezing Arctic. Polar bears stand along the edge of an ice sheet, waiting for a seal in the water to come up for air.

CANADIAN LYNX

This cat's large furry feet allow it to silently stalk snowshoe hares.

The **animals** that **predators eat** are called **prey.**

AFRICAN WILD DOG

These predators live in a pack. After a hunt, the adults throw up meat to feed the pups.

WOLF

Wolves hunt in packs to catch big animals like moose and small animals like rabbits.

115

SUPER MARSUPIALS

Marsupials are a special type of mammal. Most marsupial moms carry their babies inside a pouch on their belly. Their babies are tiny at birth—about the size of a gummy bear!

Unlike kangaroos, **quokkas** can **climb** up a **tree trunk** to reach **food.**

QUOKKA

These small marsupials leap through bushes and grass to find leaves and berries to eat. Quokkas often sleep during the heat of the day.

KOALA

A baby koala stays in its mother's pouch until it is big enough to ride on her back. The mom and baby move through the trees together looking for leaves to eat.

WOMBAT

Wombats love to dig in the dirt! They use their sharp claws and strong legs to build their homes, called burrows, underground.

BANDICOOT

Bandicoots use their pointy noses to find bugs underground. The holes they leave behind are called snout pokes.

OPOSSUM

Opossums eat almost anything, from mice and worms to food from people's trash cans! They use their long tail to hold on to branches and to carry grass for building a nest.

KANGAROO

A newborn kangaroo drinks its mother's milk inside her pouch. After about four months, the baby climbs out and makes its first hops.

HOOFING IT!

All of these four-legged mammals have a hard, fingernail-like covering called a hoof on the bottom of each foot. Hooves help animals do things like run, jump, dig, or hang on to rocks.

MOOSE

In the winter, moose use their hooves to scrape away snow to eat the grasses underneath.

BISON

This member of the cow family has a thick, shaggy coat and sharp, curved horns.

NUBIAN IBEX

An ibex's hooves work like suction cups to help it grip steep rocky cliffs.

WHITE-TAILED DEER

This deer may stomp its hooves, snort, and flash the underside of its white tail to warn other deer of danger nearby.

GIRAFFE

A giraffe's hooves are about the size of a dinner plate! A single kick can kill a lion.

TAPIR

A tapir uses its long nose to grab leaves off branches or find fruit on the ground. When it swims, a tapir uses its nose like a snorkel!

DID YOU KNOW? Giraffes are the tallest land animals!

ZEBRA

No two zebras look exactly alike. Each one has its own unique pattern of black and white stripes.

RHINOCEROS

A rhino baby, called a calf, can walk an hour after it is born.

GOLDEN-HEADED LION TAMARIN

AYE-AYE

PLAYFUL PRIMATES

Humans are primates, too!

These mammals can be big or small, but they all have thumbs that can bend. This allows them to grab things with their hands.

MANDRILL

CHIMPANZEE

MOUNTAIN GORILLA

RHESUS MACAQUES

ORANGUTANS

Most primates live in groups.

GEOFFROY'S SPIDER MONKEY

121

THE SAVANNA

All kinds of animals—big and small, predator and prey—gather at rivers and other watery spots in the African savanna. Elephants, giraffes, zebras, lions, birds, and more come to drink and cool off in the water.

Red-Billed Oxpecker
This bird perches on rhinoceroses and giraffes to eat insects off their skin.

rhinoceros

zebra

ostrich

hippo

turtle

Turtles sit atop a hippo's back to warm up in the sun.

Hippopotamus
Open wide! A hippo has the largest mouth of any land animal.

Gray Crowned Crane
These birds stomp their feet to bring insects up from the ground. Then they quickly catch and eat them.

Kirby's Dropwing
Like all dragonflies, this one has four wings that can flap fast!

Lion
These big cats live in family groups called prides. Female lions hunt and raise cubs together.

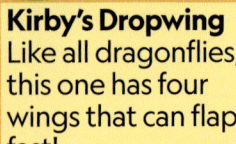

Ostriches alert zebras, which don't have very good eyesight, **when lions are nearby.**

Leopard
Leopards are good climbers! These big cats rest in tree branches during the heat of the day.

Termite
These insects carry soil from underground to build large dirt mounds on the savanna.

Warthog
These members of the pig family use their long lower teeth to defend themselves against predators like lions, hyenas, and leopards.

Spotted Hyena
These mammals make a sound like laughter after they catch prey. It's their way of telling other hyenas that dinner is ready!

alligator

giraffe

elephant

123

IN THE SEA

Most mammals live on land, but many also live in the ocean. They come to the water's surface or onto land to breathe air. Baby sea mammals drink their mother's milk.

BLUE WHALE

The blue whale is the largest animal on Earth, but it eats one of the smallest animals in the sea. A blue whale can eat millions of krill, a type of tiny shrimp, in one day!

SEA OTTER

A sea otter mom wraps her baby in seaweed to keep the pup from floating away while she dives for food.

MANATEE

Manatees are sometimes called sea cows because they are big, eat a lot of grasses, and move slowly.

NARWHAL

This mammal is nicknamed the unicorn of the sea! The male has a long spiraled tooth called a tusk that sticks out of its upper lip.

WALRUS

A walrus uses its long tusks to pull itself out of the water and onto the ice. A thick layer of fat called blubber helps keep a walrus warm in its freezing Arctic home.

Walruses and **seals** both have **front** and **rear flippers**. They can **swim** in the ocean and **walk** on land.

SEAL

Seals hunt for fish in the ocean. Some seals can hold their breath for two hours and dive deep to find food.

 # ON THE FARM

Moo! Oink! Quack! Come on down to the farm! Farms are places where people grow food and other crops. You can find lots of different animals on a farm.

Chickens are one of the closest living relatives to *Tyrannosaurus rex*.

PIG

Pigs can't sweat like people do, so they roll in mud to cool off. The mud also sticks to their skin and protects them from the sun.

GOAT

Goats can climb trees to pull off leaves. They have a four-part stomach, which helps them digest the tough vines and bushes they eat.

CHICKEN

Chickens have wings and fluffy feathers, but they can only fly a very short distance.

DUCK

Ducks use their webbed feet like paddles to help them swim. And their downy feathers trap air so that they can stay warm and float on water.

COW

Large eyes allow cows to see almost all the way around themselves without moving their heads. This helps them see in all directions when their heads are down grazing on grass.

HORSE

A newborn horse, or foal, can sleep 12 hours per day. Adult horses sleep only about five hours per day. They can even sleep standing up!

Sheep are social! They like to live in groups, or flocks.

SHEEP

A domestic sheep's wool never stops growing. People trim it off and use it to make things like sweaters and blankets.

127

FASCINATING BIRDS

Birds are a group of animals that hatch from eggs. They have feathers. Most birds use their wings to fly. Their beaks help them dig for bugs, break open seeds, or even catch fish.

RHINOCEROS HORNBILL

This bird uses the brightly colored horn on its beak to show off to other birds.

NORTHERN CARDINAL

Male cardinals, which are red, sing to impress female cardinals. The females build their nests with twigs, grass, and leaves.

VULTURE

These birds are nature's cleanup crew! Vultures eat animals that have already died. This helps keep the environment clean.

GOLDEN EAGLE

These large birds swoop down to grab rabbits, ground squirrels, and other prey with their sharp claws, called talons.

GREAT BLUE HERON

This tall bird wades into shallow water and waits for a fish to swim by. Then the heron uses its long bill to quickly snatch its meal.

PUFFIN

These sea birds fly and swim! Puffins paddle fast through the water with their wings, diving to catch small fish.

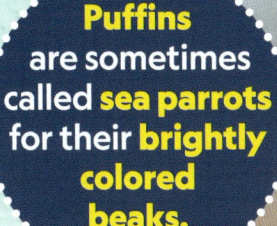

Puffins are sometimes called sea parrots for their brightly colored beaks.

HUMMINGBIRD

This small bird beats its wings so fast it can hover in midair like a helicopter! A hummingbird can also fly backward and upside down.

SHOW-OFFS

These male birds show off their brightly colored feathers to attract a mate.

LADY AMHERST PHEASANT

These birds can fly but mostly walk on the ground looking for insects, seeds, and roots to eat.

SUMMER TANAGER

These bright red birds also sing a pretty song to get females to notice them.

PEACOCK

A peacock's long tail feathers usually trail behind him. But when he wants to get a female's attention, he fans out his flashy feathers and dances!

GOULDIAN FINCH

These birds flock together in leafy trees to stay cool in the shade. A male bobs his head and ruffles his bright purple feathers to catch the eye of a female.

WILSON'S BIRD OF PARADISE

This bird stands out with his curled tail feathers and bright colors. It is only found on two small islands.

HUNTERS

Big birds like hawks and falcons are fierce hunters. They use their sharp talons to snatch prey. Some small birds are hunters, too. They catch a lot of bugs and worms in their beaks.

PEREGRINE FALCON

Peregrine falcons are the fastest animals on Earth. They can dive for their prey at more than 200 miles an hour (320 km/h)—as fast as a race car!

BLACK-WINGED KITE

This bird flaps its wings to stay in one place in the air as it looks for mice on the ground below.

ROBIN

These songbirds use their strong senses of sight and hearing to find worms. Robins tug hard with their beaks to pull their wiggly prey from the dirt!

OWL

Owls hunt at night, using their excellent hearing to find prey. They fly so quietly that their prey can't hear them coming.

RED-TAILED HAWK

Hawks fly in circles high in the air. When they see a rabbit or a snake moving in the grass below, they swoop down to grab it.

LONG-EARED OWL

131

WHO, ME? FLY?

Don't look to the sky to find these birds. They have feathers, but they can't fly.

EMPEROR PENGUIN

The world's biggest penguins huddle together on Antarctica's icy land. The group protects each other from freezing cold winds.

Emperor penguins have tight, thick layers of waterproof feathers that help keep them warm and dry.

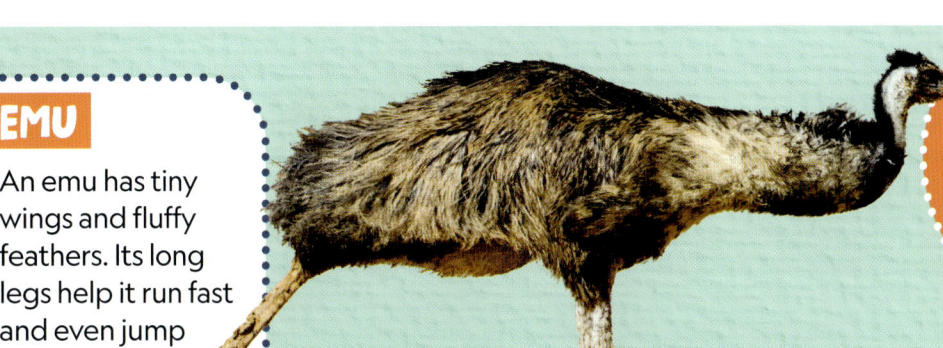

EMU

An emu has tiny wings and fluffy feathers. Its long legs help it run fast and even jump super high.

Emus protect themselves from predators with their **powerful kick.**

KAKAPO

This parrot climbs tall trees to find fruit. At night, the bird looks for leaves and roots on the ground.

KIWI

A kiwi's long, curved beak has nostrils on the tip! It pokes into leaves on the forest floor to sniff out earthworms, snails, and berries.

OSTRICH

Meet the heaviest and tallest bird on Earth! An ostrich spreads its wings to help it balance when running. And it runs fast—up to 43 miles an hour (69 km/h)!

SOUTHERN CASSOWARY

The tall hornlike bump on the top of this bird's head is called a casque. It is made of the same material as human fingernails.

THE RAINFOREST

Tropical rainforests in Central and South America are filled with trees and plants that grow close together. A rainforest has four levels, or layers. Each layer is like a neighborhood where different kinds of plants and animals live.

Jamaican fruit bat

blue morpho butterfly

It rains almost every day in a tropical rainforest.

scarlet macaw

howler monkey

harpy eagle

pink-toed tarantula

emperor tamarin

two-toed sloth

EMERGENT LAYER

This top layer is made up of the tallest treetops that reach toward the sky. Animals that fly and glide live here.

CANOPY

Tree leaves and branches form a giant green roof for the forest below. Animals that live in this layer make loud calls so they can hear each other through the leaves.

toco toucan

crimson topaz hummingbird

leafcutter ant

About half of Earth's plants and animals live in rainforests.

tamandua

great curassow

jaguar

Brazilian rainbow boa

red-footed tortoise

red-eyed tree frog

Hercules beetle

UNDERSTORY

This layer is filled with small trees and vines. Some animals rest in the trees, waiting to pounce or slither down to catch prey on the forest floor.

FOREST FLOOR

The forest floor is covered in roots and fallen leaves. This dark and shady bottom layer is a great hiding place for small rodents, insects, and worms.

capybara

millipede

REMARKABLE REPTILES

Snakes, turtles, lizards, alligators, and crocodiles are all reptiles. Most reptiles hatch from eggs. Baby reptiles look like their parents—just smaller! Their dry skin is covered with scales or bony plates.

GOLD DUST DAY GECKO

If a predator grabs this lizard's tail, the tail falls off! Then the gecko runs away. It grows a new tail in about three weeks.

FIJI BANDED IGUANA

This lizard moves from tree to tree in the highest branches. Its green and pale blue stripes help it blend in with the leaves and sky.

LOGGERHEAD SEA TURTLE

Female sea turtles go back to the beach where they were born to lay their eggs in the sand. When the baby sea turtles hatch, they scurry into the ocean and swim away.

KING COBRA

This long snake bites its prey with tiny fangs that deliver deadly venom. Some cobras can spit their venom.

THORNY DEVIL

This desert reptile is covered with spiky scales that keep most predators from getting too close.

Chameleons can change their skin color!

DID YOU KNOW?

Chameleons can look in two different directions at once.

PANTHER CHAMELEON

A chameleon doesn't move very fast, but its tongue does! This lizard can shoot its long tongue out of its mouth faster than a sports car to catch bugs to eat.

SNAKES AND LIZARDS

Many lizards have long bodies, with four legs and a tail that help them crawl and climb. Snakes don't have legs, but they can still slither with speed!

GREEN BASILISK

This lizard can run on water! Flaps of skin on its back feet spread out so the lizard can sprint across the water's surface.

KOMODO DRAGON

Meet the world's biggest lizard! It hunts large animals, like deer, wild pigs, and water buffalo.

NOSY HARA LEAF CHAMELEON

This tiny lizard could fit on your fingernail! It uses its tail to help it climb up trees. It sleeps in the branches at night.

Snakes shed their **skin** as they **grow.** The old skin comes off in one long piece. Under it is **new skin.**

EYELASH PALM PIT VIPER

Most snakes have smooth scales, but this pit viper's are sharp. It's named for the scales above its eyes that look like eyelashes.

BOA CONSTRICTOR

This thick snake wraps itself around prey and squeezes before swallowing it whole. It can live off one meal for weeks.

CORN SNAKE

A corn snake is sometimes called a red rat snake. It slithers through underground burrows looking for mice and rats to eat.

Corn snakes are constrictors, too!

BEARDED DRAGON

This lizard has a "beard" of spikes under its chin. It can puff up its spiky skin to scare off predators.

TURTLES AND CROCS

These reptiles walk on land or swim in the water. Some do both! Turtles do not have teeth. They use their beaks to crush their food. Alligators and crocodiles have lots of teeth!

The **Galápagos giant tortoise** is the **world's largest tortoise.**

AMERICAN ALLIGATOR

A mother alligator lays her eggs in a nest she builds on land. After the babies hatch, she gently carries them in her mouth to the water.

GALÁPAGOS GIANT TORTOISE

Thick, sturdy legs hold up this huge and heavy reptile, but it still spends a lot of time lying down. These tortoises rest for about 16 hours every day.

LEATHERBACK SEA TURTLE

This turtle lives most of its life in the ocean. It does not have a hard shell. It has tough, rubbery skin instead.

EASTERN BOX TURTLE

A box turtle can close up tight like a box! When a predator gets too close, the turtle pulls in its head, legs, and tail. Then it snaps shut its shell. Box turtles are often found near ponds or streams.

NILE CROCODILE

This large reptile mostly eats fish. Sometimes, Nile crocodiles use their strong tail to burst straight up out of the water to grab a zebra or small hippo on land.

Nile crocodiles live in rivers, marshes, and swamps in Africa.

THE DESERT

A desert is a place that gets very little rain. Here are some animals and plants that you might see in the southwestern United States. They can survive without much water.

Desert plants store water in their thick stems.

Kit Fox
These mammals have fur on their paw pads to protect them from the hot sand.

saguaro cactus

Cactus Wren
These birds build nests in the spines of a cactus or shrub.

cholla cactus

Common Chuckwalla
This reptile can puff itself up to wedge its body between rocks. This helps tuck it away from predators.

Desert Tortoise
These reptiles use their short legs and long claws to dig burrows, where they hide away from the heat.

queen butterfly

Some desert plants only bloom when it rains.

Desert Bighorn Sheep
These mammals use their horns to break open and eat a barrel cactus.

Coyote
These mammals are nicknamed "song dogs" because their loud howls can be heard from far away.

Black-Tailed Jackrabbit
This mammal's long ears help it keep cool in the hot desert.

Mojave Rattlesnake
This reptile shakes its tail to make a buzzing sound that warns predators away.

barrel cactus

Roadrunner
These birds love to run! A pair of roadrunners work as a team to kill a rattlesnake.

143

AMAZING AMPHIBIANS

Frogs, toads, and salamanders belong to a group of animals called amphibians. They hatch from eggs. Most amphibians live close to water to keep their skin moist.

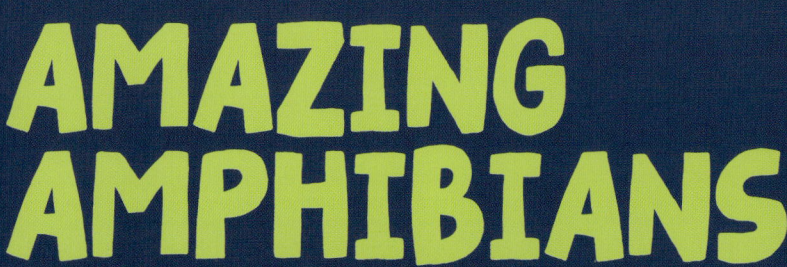

COMMON TOAD

Toads are a kind of frog. They have dry, bumpy skin. They live on land and use their sticky tongue to catch prey.

Most **frogs have teeth,** but toads do not.

ORIENTAL FIRE-BELLIED TOAD

This toad flips over to show predators its bright red belly. The color is a warning that the toad's skin is poisonous.

TIGER SALAMANDER

The largest salamander on land digs burrows near the water. It comes out at night to hunt for worms, insects, and even other amphibians.

CALIFORNIA NEWT

Newts are a kind of salamander with rougher skin. The California newt's skin makes a poison that can stun or kill a predator.

Axolotls use their **mouth** like a **suction cup** to inhale worms, tadpoles, and insects.

AXOLOTL

Unlike other salamanders, axolotls never leave the water. These salamanders have a special superpower, too. If their limbs or organs get hurt, they can grow new ones!

BLUE-SIDED TREE FROG

This rainforest frog hunts for insects in the trees at night. It sleeps on green leaves during the day, tucking in to hide its colorful feet and underside from hungry birds and snakes.

FROGS GROW UP

Frogs undergo an awesome change as they grow from an egg to a grown-up. This change is called metamorphosis. Watch how a frog transforms!

EGGS

Most mother frogs lay their eggs in or near water.

TADPOLES

When the eggs hatch, out pop tadpoles! A tadpole has a tail that helps it swim underwater.

LOOK, LEGS!

The tadpole gets bigger and bigger. It sprouts legs for swimming and hopping.

GOODBYE, TAIL

The tadpole's tail gets smaller and smaller. Its eyes get bulgier and bulgier.

Frog eggs are laid in **clumps**. **Toad** eggs are laid in **strings**.

Tadpoles are also called **pollywogs**. They live **underwater** and eat **tiny plants**.

HELLO, FROG

Finally, the tadpole looks like a frog. It crawls out of the water. Now it's a grown-up. *Ribbit!*

RED-EYED TREE FROG

FANTASTIC FISH

Fish of all shapes, colors, and sizes swim in oceans, lakes, and rivers. Fish are covered with scales. They breathe with special organs called gills. Fish hatch from eggs.

MORAY EEL

This long fish uses its sharp teeth to catch other fish and octopuses. Some moray eels have another set of teeth hidden inside their throat!

Moray eels **hide** along **rocky shorelines** and **in coral reefs**.

RAINBOW TROUT

This fish lives in rivers and streams. Its pretty colors shine when it jumps high out of the water.

NURSE SHARK

Nurse sharks pile on top of each other on the ocean floor during the day. They hunt for lobsters, small stingrays, squid, and fish at night.

SAILFISH

This is the fastest fish in the sea! It can sail out of the water at high speed, too. It gets its name from its tall fin that it can raise and lower like a ship's sail.

LEAFY SEADRAGON

The leafy seadragon has frilly fins that help it blend in with seaweed in the ocean.

YELLOW-HEADED JAWFISH

This fish uses its big mouth to dig a burrow in the ocean floor. If a predator gets too close, it dives into this safer spot in the sand.

SEAHORSE

This fish holds on to corals and seagrasses with its tail. It waits for prey to pass by. Then the seahorse uses its long snout to suck up the food in one gulp.

SWORDFISH

Soon after it hatches, a swordfish already has a visible bill. This speedy swimmer swings its sharp bill, or sword, back and forth to catch its prey.

149

GREAT WHITE SHARK

SPECTACULAR SHARKS

Sharks have been swimming the world's oceans since before dinosaurs roamed Earth. There are more than 500 kinds of these fierce fish.

CAT SHARK

HAMMERHEAD SHARK

WHALE SHARK

TIGER SHARK

Whale sharks, the world's largest shark, prey only on small fish.

GOBLIN SHARK

SHORTFIN MAKO SHARK

LEMON SHARK

OCEAN ZONES

More than three-quarters of Earth is covered by one big ocean. Its salty waters are home to most of the living things on Earth.

Top to Bottom

There are four different zones, or layers, of the ocean. Sunlight fades as the water gets deeper. The ocean gets darker. It also gets colder.

SUNLIGHT ZONE

Sunlight shines down from the water's surface. It provides light and warmth for plants and animals. Sea plants, such as kelp and seaweed, need the sun to grow.

TWILIGHT ZONE

Very little sunlight travels to the twilight zone. There is barely enough sun for sea plants to grow.

MIDNIGHT ZONE

There is no sunlight this far beneath the ocean's surface. That means it is dark and cold all the time.

ABYSSAL ZONE

Mountains, volcanoes, deep valleys, canyons, and huge, flat plains are found on the seafloor.

HAMMERHEAD SHARK

GIANT OCTOPUS

GULPER EEL

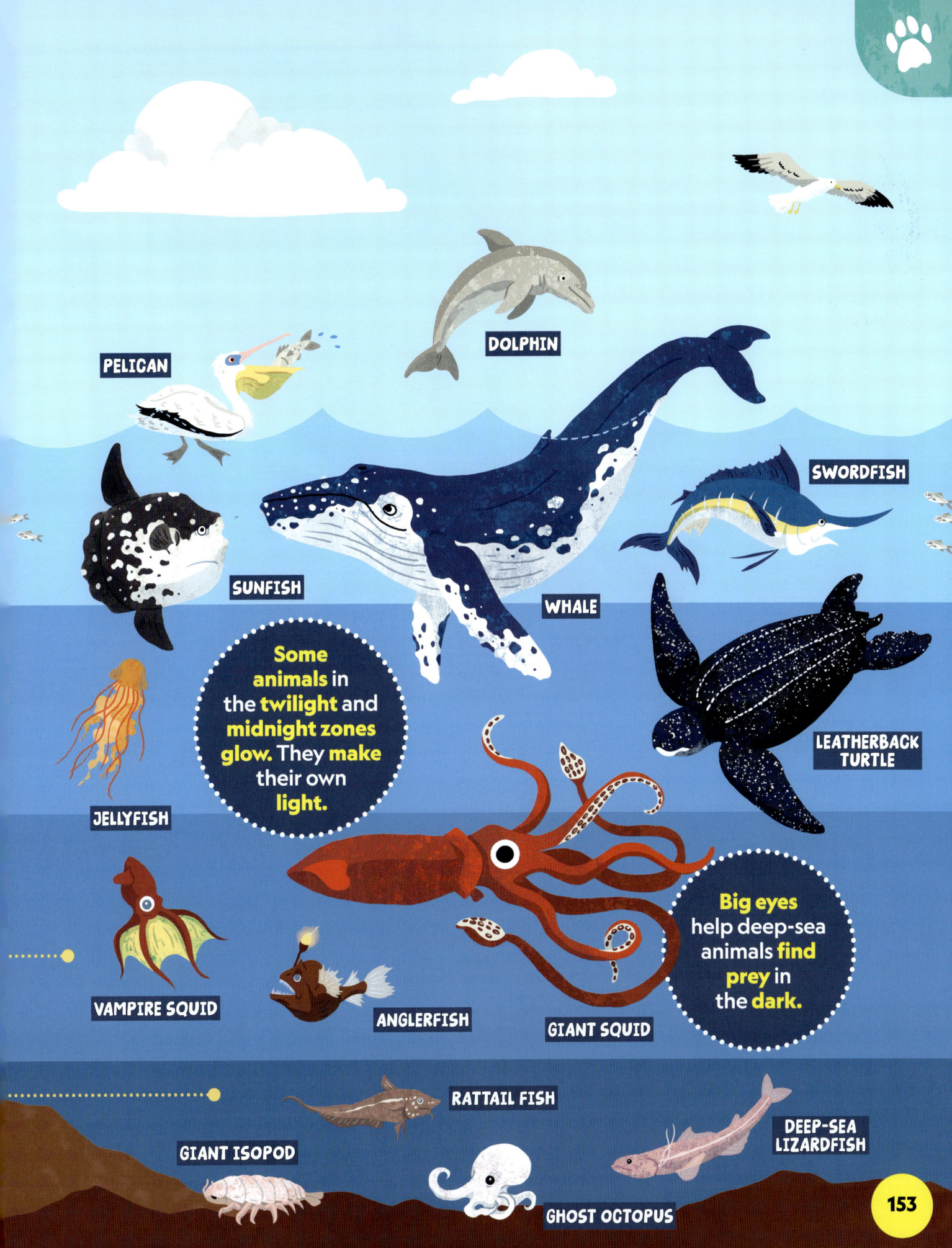

PELICAN

DOLPHIN

SWORDFISH

SUNFISH

WHALE

LEATHERBACK TURTLE

Some animals in the twilight and midnight zones glow. They make their own light.

JELLYFISH

Big eyes help deep-sea animals find prey in the dark.

VAMPIRE SQUID

ANGLERFISH

GIANT SQUID

RATTAIL FISH

DEEP-SEA LIZARDFISH

GIANT ISOPOD

GHOST OCTOPUS

AWESOME INVERTEBRATES

Animals that do not have a backbone are called invertebrates. They live on land and in water.

Most of the **animals** on Earth are **invertebrates.**

MIMIC OCTOPUS

This small octopus hides at night. During the day, it changes into the shape of different sea creatures to stay safe while it searches for food.

CROWN JELLYFISH

Jellyfish do not have brains, hearts, bones, or blood. Long, thin tentacles hang from an umbrella-shaped body called a bell.

GARDEN SNAIL

This tiny land animal has a hard shell that it can hide inside. Its soft body is covered with slime that helps it scoot across the ground.

MILLIPEDE

This creepy-crawly has a lot of legs, but it can't move fast to escape a predator. It coils its body into a tight spiral to protect its soft underside.

RAINBOW SCARAB

This beautiful beetle tunnels through—and eats!—poop that mammals leave behind.

EARTHWORM

These worms mix the dirt as they wiggle down deep. This helps make the dirt a good place for plants to grow.

VAMPIRE SQUID

The vampire squid lives in the deep ocean, where it is very dark. It has big eyes and tiny lights at the tips of its arms to help it see.

PEACOCK MANTIS SHRIMP

This shrimp uses one of its front claws to quickly punch its prey. The strike is 50 times faster than the blink of a human eye!

INSECTS

An insect, like a beetle or a bee, has six legs and three main body parts: head, thorax, and abdomen. Most of them have wings and antennae.

HOUSE ANT

You might see these tiny insects crawling where you live. They'll scurry toward anything sweet that's left lying around.

An insect uses its antennae to smell and to taste.

HONEYBEE

These bees make honey. They live together in groups called colonies that can have as many as 60,000 busy bees.

LUNA MOTH

A caterpillar hatches from a tiny egg. It munches on leaves and grows bigger. Then it makes a cocoon. In a few weeks, a big green moth comes out!

PRAYING MANTIS

This insect sits very still. Then ZAP! Its legs shoot out fast and grab a bug to eat. Its front legs have rows of sharp spines to help it hold on to its prey.

ARACHNIDS

An arachnid, like a spider or a scorpion, has eight legs and two main body parts: head and abdomen. It has no wings.

PEACOCK SPIDER

Let's dance! A male peacock spider fans out its colorful body, waves its legs, and dances to impress a female.

WOLF SPIDER

Most wolf spiders don't spin webs to catch insects. They chase and pounce on their prey, just like the animal they are named for.

SCORPION

This arachnid has a tail with a sharp stinger on the end. The scorpion quickly grabs prey with its pincers. Then it whips the poisonous tip of its tail forward to sting its insect meal.

WRITING SPIDER

This large black-and-yellow spider spins a strong web with thick zigzags that look like writing. It waits at the center of the web for insects to get caught in the sticky strands.

WINGING IT

Some insect wings are easy to spot. But some insect wings are hidden—until it's time to fly!

The **dragonfly's enormous eyes** help it **watch** for **prey.**

DRAGONFLY

A dragonfly flaps its four wings fast to move in all directions. It catches insects to eat while it's flying!

GREEN STINK BUG

The X pattern formed by this bug's folded wings warns predators "Don't touch!" Stink bugs spray a smelly liquid when in danger.

LADYBUG

Beetles, like this ladybug, have two sets of wings. The back wings are used for flying.

FIREFLY

When these beetles fly, they flash a light. Fireflies "talk" to each other with this light. The color of a firefly's glow can range from red to yellow to green.

BUTTERFLY

Butterflies flutter from flower to flower with large wings. They sip a sweet liquid called nectar from the blooms.

HOUSEFLY

A housefly's wings let it fly in spirals, zigzags, and even backward. It has a tiny second set of wings that help it balance while in the air.

CICADA

Male cicadas are noisy! They rub their wings together and use a special body part on their belly to make loud buzzing and clicking sounds.

GRASSHOPPER

These insects use their strong back legs to spring into the air. Then they use their wings to fly. Grasshoppers also rub their front wings against their back legs to make chirping sounds.

INSIDE AN ANTHILL

Thousands of tiny ants work together to create an amazing nest.

DOORS

Ants move in and out of small openings they make in the mound. They may block these "doorways" with small pebbles or bits of wood.

WORKER

A worker ant gathers food, protects baby ants, and takes care of the nest.

TUNNELS

Worker ants dig tunnels to connect the chambers, or rooms. The dirt they dig out creates the mound.

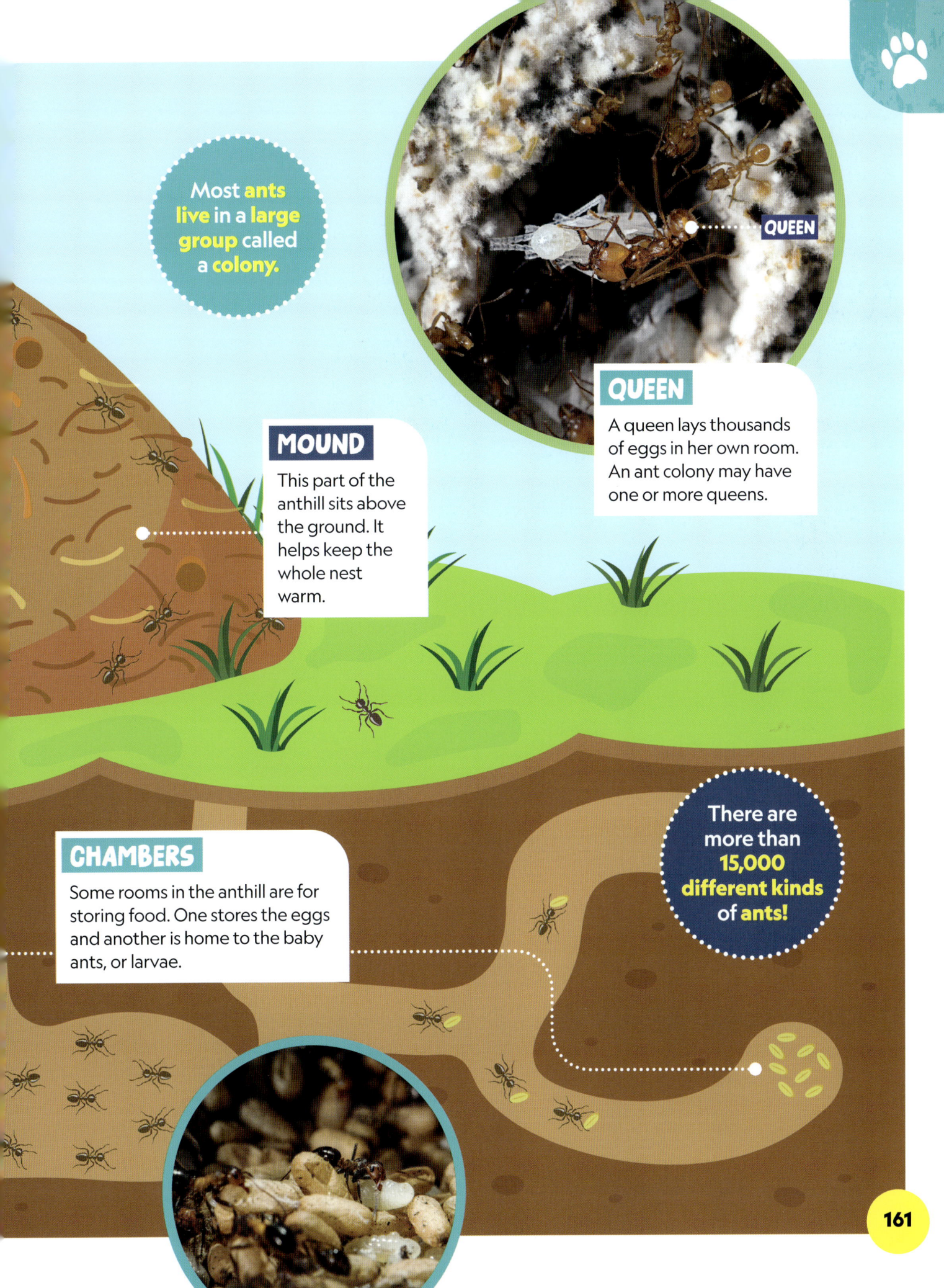

Most **ants live** in a **large group** called a **colony.**

QUEEN

QUEEN

A queen lays thousands of eggs in her own room. An ant colony may have one or more queens.

MOUND

This part of the anthill sits above the ground. It helps keep the whole nest warm.

There are more than **15,000 different kinds** of **ants!**

CHAMBERS

Some rooms in the anthill are for storing food. One stores the eggs and another is home to the baby ants, or larvae.

THAT'S COOL!

CLEVER CAMOUFLAGE

SLOTH

ARCTIC FOX

BIRD-DROPPING SPIDER

YELLOWLINE ARROW CRAB

TIGER

CRAB SPIDER

WALKING LEAF

THORN MIMIC TREEHOPPERS

ADDER SNAKE

CHAPTER 6

Dino-ROAR!

Millions of years ago, long before there were **any people, dinosaurs** and other **creatures large** and small **roamed Earth's land,** seas, and **skies.**

165

DINO TIMES

Dinosaurs lived on Earth during a time called the Mesozoic era. The Mesozoic era is divided into three periods. The land on Earth looked different during each of these periods.

CRYOLOPHOSAURUS

The **earliest** known bird, *Archaeopteryx,* took to the skies in the **late Jurassic.**

TRIASSIC PERIOD
(252–201 MILLION YEARS AGO)

Hello, dinos! Dinosaurs and other reptiles appeared when most of Earth was hot and looked like a desert.

NYASASAURUS

JURASSIC PERIOD
(201–145 MILLION YEARS AGO)

Dinos dominate! Some of the biggest animals ever to live were the dinosaurs of the Jurassic period. Earth changed from hot and dry to warm and wet. Evergreen trees spread across the land.

Ferns were the main **plants** on land when dinos first **roamed.**

HUALIANCERATOPS

DID YOU KNOW?

Dinosaurs were reptiles. Reptiles living today include crocodiles, snakes, and turtles.

GUANLONG

CRETACEOUS PERIOD
(145–66 MILLION YEARS AGO)

New types of dinosaurs like *Triceratops* and *Tyrannosaurus rex* shared the land with many different kinds of birds and mammals. Insects from bees to beetles helped spread the first flowering plants.

PATAGOTITAN

MEET SOME MEAT-EATERS

Meat-eating dinosaurs had powerful jaws and sharp, curved teeth that were perfect for cutting through prey.

ALLOSAURUS
(LATE JURASSIC)

This dinosaur grabbed prey with huge claws that were shaped like hooks.

MICRORAPTOR
(EARLY CRETACEOUS)

The long feathers on this dino's arms and legs may have helped it glide from tree to tree.

Scientists think that *Microraptor* had shiny **black feathers,** like a crow.

Microraptor had a **long, bony tail** with feathers on the end.

COELOPHYSIS
(LATE TRIASSIC)

This early dinosaur was lightweight, long, and fast. Its long tail helped it balance and steer when it ran.

GIGANOTOSAURUS
(EARLY CRETACEOUS)

This fierce meat-eater had long teeth that it used to slice into prey.

DEINONYCHUS
(EARLY CRETACEOUS)

This small dino may have hunted in packs. A long, curved claw on each foot was its main weapon.

SPINOSAURUS
(LATE CRETACEOUS)

This huge predator lived on land but hunted fish in rivers and swamps. The sail on its back had tall, bony spines.

TYRANNOSAURUS REX
(LATE CRETACEOUS)

T. rex had the strongest bite of any land animal ever! This big dino could chew right through bone!

HELLO, PLANT-EATERS!

The biggest dinosaurs ate only plants. Their flat teeth were made for chomping leaves and branches.

STEGOSAURUS
(LATE JURASSIC)

Scientists think this dinosaur used the large plates on its back to attract a mate.

IGUANODON
(EARLY CRETACEOUS)

Iguanodon was about the size of an African elephant. Each of its front hands had a sharp thumb spike and a finger that could hold things.

This dino could trot on two legs!

Like all **reptiles**, dinosaurs **hatched** from eggs.

PARASAUROLOPHUS
(LATE CRETACEOUS)

This plant-eater likely used its head crest like a trumpet to communicate with its herd.

TRICERATOPS
(LATE CRETACEOUS)

This dino's sharp beak could cut through tough plants. It used its massive teeth to grind them up.

ANKYLOSAURUS
(LATE CRETACEOUS)

Hundreds of bony plates protected this dinosaur. It used the huge club on the end of its tail to fight off predators.

APATOSAURUS
(LATE JURASSIC)

This dinosaur's eggs were the size of soccer balls.

Even the **eyelids** of *Ankylosaurus* were **covered** with **armor!**

SUPERSAURUS
(LATE JURASSIC)

This dino is the longest ever discovered. It was longer than three school buses in a row!

IN THE SKY

When dinosaurs roamed the land, flying reptiles soared through the sky.

The **birds** we see **today** are some of the closest **living relatives** of the dinosaurs.

PTERANODON
(LATE CRETACEOUS)

These fliers had hollow bones to keep them lightweight. A kind of fur on their bodies kept them warm. They scooped fish out of the water with their beaks.

Scientists think *Pteranodon* was very **colorful,** just like **birds today.**

HATZEGOPTERYX
(LATE CRETACEOUS)

This pterosaur could swoop from the sky and pick up a dinosaur the size of a pony with its gigantic beak.

NEMICOLOPTERUS
(EARLY CRETACEOUS)

This pterosaur was about the size of a robin. Its wings were made of skin stretched between one long finger and the side of its body.

IN THE SEA

Reptiles ruled the ocean, too! These large creatures swam among sharks, other fish, and squid.

SARCOSUCHUS
(EARLY CRETACEOUS)

This distant relative of today's crocodile was as long as a bus! This reptile chomped on everything from fish to dinosaurs.

ARCHELON
(LATE CRETACEOUS)

This early sea turtle was nearly the size of a small car.

PLESIOSAURUS
(EARLY JURASSIC)

Plesiosaurus used its flippers to move its wide body through the water. This reptile stretched its long neck to search for prey.

OPHTHALMOSAURUS
(LATE JURASSIC)

This reptile's huge eyes let it see well even in the deep, dark ocean. Like a dolphin, it came to the surface to breathe.

MOSASAURUS
(LATE CRETACEOUS)

This enormous reptile could chomp down on a shark with its two rows of teeth, then swallow it whole.

DISCOVERING DINOSAURS

How do we know so much about dinosaurs? Fossils! Fossils are the remains of living things that can be found in rocks. They can be shells, bones, teeth, footprints—even a whole skeleton!

When a species **dies out** completely, it is said to be **extinct.**

A SCIENTIST USES A PICKAX TO UNCOVER FOSSILS.

DIGGING DEEP

Paleontologists are scientists who study fossils. They are like detectives. They search for clues in areas where wind and rain have worn away rocks. If they spot a shape that looks like it could be a fossil, they use small tools to carefully push away the dirt and rock around it.

I SEE YOU!

Fossils can tell scientists the size of a dinosaur, what it ate, and how it moved.

FOSSIL OF A FEATHER

SURPRISE!

Fossils have shown us that some dinosaurs had scaly skin, like most reptiles do. But a fossil found in China showed that some dinosaurs had feathers!

FAMOUS FOSSIL FIND

About 200 years ago, a young girl named Mary Anning helped her father look for fossils on the beach in England. When she was about 12 years old, her brother found a fossil that looked like a monster's skull. Mary spent months digging out the fossil. It was a complete *Ichthyosaurus* skeleton, more than 17 feet (5.2 m) long!

MARY ANNING

PLIOSAUR FOSSIL FOUND BY MARY ANNING

What Happened to the Dinosaurs?

Most scientists think that dinosaurs and other creatures disappeared 66 million years ago when a giant space rock called an asteroid hit Earth. The crash created a huge dust cloud that made the skies grow dark. Without sunlight, much of life on Earth died out.

Animals such as **jellyfish, sharks, and insects survived** after the **asteroid hit.**

HOW FOSSILS FORM

It can take millions of years for a once living dinosaur to become a fossil that scientists can dig out from the dirt. Let's follow the footsteps of a *Triceratops* and go fossil hunting!

Two male *Triceratops* lock horns, fighting to impress a female *Triceratops*.

The winner walks away. The other male *Triceratops* is badly wounded, and it dies.

Over time, its body gets covered with layers of mud and sand.

Even More Fossils

Bones are not the only things that can become fossils. Footprints, tooth marks, nests, eggshells, and leaves can fossilize, too. Even poop can become a fossil!

Dinosaur fossils have been found on every continent.

Its bones slowly turn to rock.

Millions of years later, these rocks are pushed to the surface, where we can see them.

A scientist explores an area where she thinks she might find dinosaur fossils. She spots a bone sticking out of the sand. Let the dig begin!

THAT'S COOL!

DINO STANDOUTS

LONGEST NAME:
MICROPACHYCEPHALOSAURUS

BIGGEST: TITANOSAURUS

ARGENTINOSAURUS, A KIND OF TITANOSAUR

LONGEST TAIL: **DIPLODOCUS**

MOST HORNS: **KOSMOCERATOPS**

MOST TEETH: **NIGERSAURUS**

LONGEST CLAWS: **THERIZINOSAURUS**

CHAPTER 7

Time Machine

People have lived on **Earth** for **millions of years.** Over those years, the **way we live** has **CHANGED** a lot!

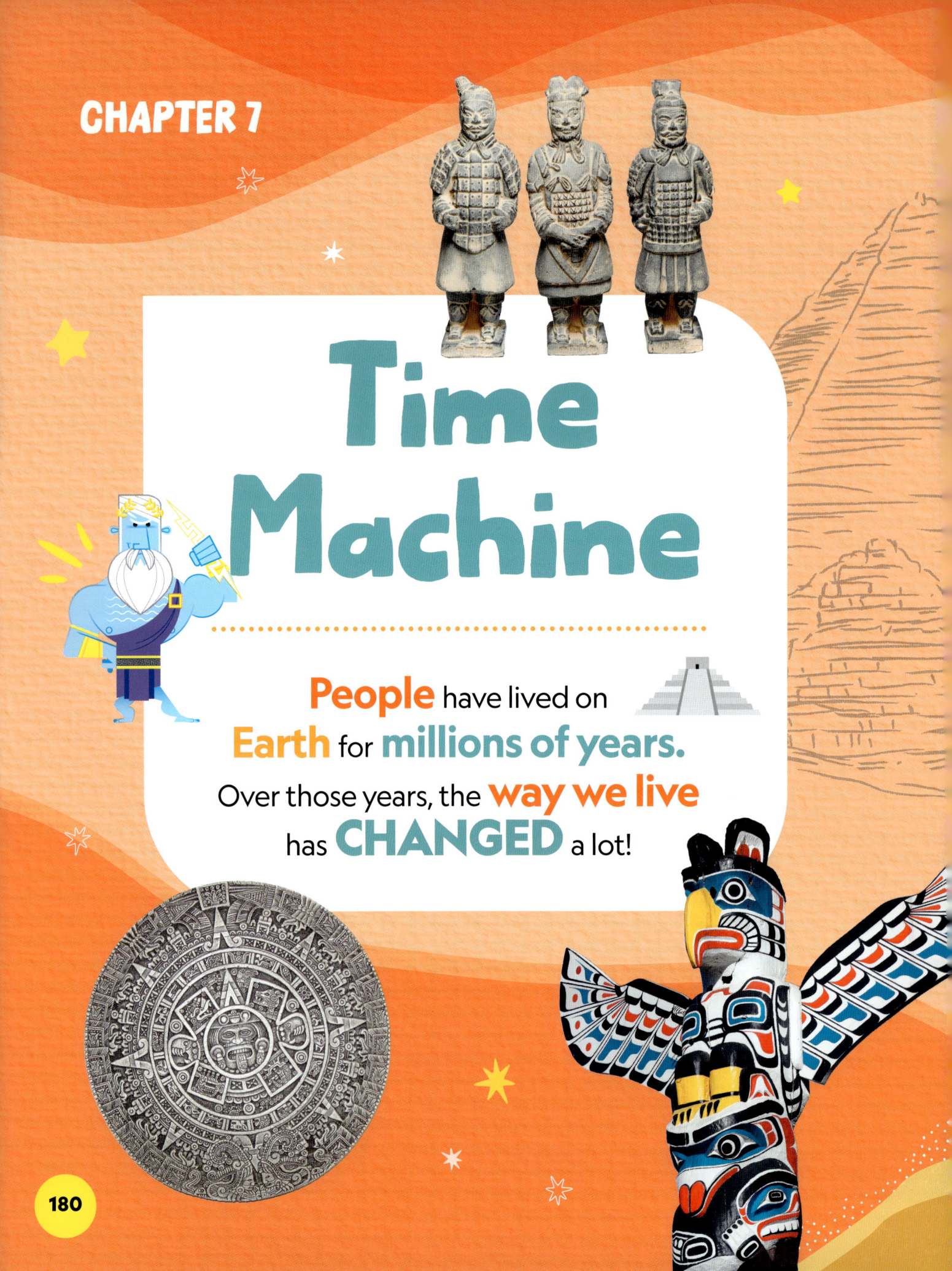

181

CLUES FROM CAVES

Many thousands of years ago, people moved around to gather fruits and nuts and to hunt animals to eat. They lived in caves or out in the open. Some made pictures in caves or on rocks. These pictures give us clues about how early humans lived.

In some places, early people carved or scratched drawings into rock.

HUNTING

Many cave or rock pictures, like this one in Utah, U.S.A., show people hunting animals for food. This hunter is using a bow and arrow.

WOOLLY MAMMOTH

This huge mammal was like a bigger elephant, with fur. People hunted it for food. Giant animals like this were called megafauna. The woolly mammoth does not exist today.

Early humans **ground up rocks** to make **black** and **red paint.**

HIGH FIVE!

Some of the oldest cave paintings are outlines of human hands, like these found in Argentina at Cueva de las Manos. That means "Cave of Hands" in Spanish.

LIVING WITH ANIMALS

Early people shared the world with a lot of different animals. Some of them looked like animals we know today, like the cow and horse in this cave painting from France.

Tool Time

People began making tools out of stone thousands of years ago. Arrowheads were used for hunting. Other stone tools were blades, spearheads, and axe heads.

SPEARHEAD

ARROWHEAD

183

WHO LIVED WHERE?

Over thousands of years, some people began to stay in one place and farm. They built towns and cities. Around the world, groups of people created their own special art, writing, and buildings. This map shows where some of these different groups, or civilizations, lived.

ANCIENT ROME

Ancient Romans were known for their strong armies. They conquered many other lands.

NATIVE NORTH AMERICANS

Long before European explorers came to North America, Native people were already living all over the land.

MAYA

Ancient Maya people created a calendar that kept track of the movements of the sun, moon, planets, and stars.

HAWAII

Native Hawaiians steered their boats across the ocean by watching the stars, sun, and winds.

INCA

The Inca grew potatoes, corn, avocados, beans, and other crops.

EASTER ISLAND (RAPA NUI)

Native people on this small island in the Pacific Ocean were expert stone carvers.

PHOENICIA

Phoenician people sailed around the Mediterranean Sea to trade with other people. They were famous for their ships and the purple cloth they made.

ARCTIC OCEAN

NORTH AMERICA

EUROPE

PACIFIC OCEAN

ATLANTIC OCEAN

AFRICA

SOUTH AMERICA

MESOPOTAMIA

The world's first towns and cities appeared in Mesopotamia. People here invented the first wheels, which were used to make pottery. They built large temples called ziggurats.

ANCIENT GREECE

Ancient Greece was divided into small city-states. Each was said to be protected by a god or goddess.

PERSIA

The Persian Empire was once one of the world's most powerful nations. It was famous for its soldiers. The lion was a symbol of royalty and power in ancient Persia.

ANCIENT CHINA

The Chinese were the first to make silk from silkworm cocoons. The process was kept secret from the rest of the world for a very long time.

ASIA

PACIFIC OCEAN

INDUS VALLEY

The Indus people were some of the first to put wheels on vehicles. They made jewelry and weapons out of copper, tin, gold, and other metals.

INDIAN OCEAN

AUSTRALIA, NEW ZEALAND, AND OCEANIA

FIRST AUSTRALIANS

Aboriginals were the first people ever to live in Australia. Storytelling, painting, and dance are important parts of Aboriginal culture.

SOUTHERN OCEAN

ANTARCTICA

ANCIENT EGYPT

People in ancient Egypt grew a lot of grain. Most people ate bread and porridge at meals.

MAORI PEOPLE

Early Maori people in New Zealand lived near the ocean. They hunted for seals and fished.

185

ANCIENT EGYPT

Towns and cities in ancient Egypt were built along the Nile River. Water from the river helped crops grow. Boats were used to move things, including giant blocks of stone for the pyramids.

KING TUT

Tutankhamun was only nine years old when he became pharaoh, or king. When he died, his mummy was placed in a room underground, called a tomb. It was filled with all the things people thought he would need in the afterlife, including jewels, food, and games.

DID YOU KNOW?

People wore jewelry in the shape of the scarab beetle, an insect thought to bring good luck.

THE SPHINX

This supersize statue with a human head and a lion's body was carved out of one huge piece of stone. More than six stories tall, it stands guard by the pyramids.

THE GREAT PYRAMID OF GIZA

It took more than two million stone blocks to build this tomb for the pharaoh Khufu.

CLEOPATRA

Cleopatra, the last queen of Egypt, fought her brother for the throne. She later led a fleet of warships to defeat a Roman rival, too.

MUMMIES

When some Egyptians died, their body was turned into a mummy. It was dried out and wrapped tightly in linen. The mummy was often decorated with a mask and placed in a painted coffin.

HIEROGLYPHS

Egyptian writing looked like pictures. Scribes painted and carved hieroglyphs to tell stories.

GODS AND GODDESSES

Ancient Egyptians believed in gods and goddesses that would bring them good fortune. Many were imagined as part human and part animal. Egyptians had gods for the sun, war, and even cats.

ANCIENT CHINA

This civilization began along the Yellow River in China. People built walls around cities to separate and protect them.

Most of the statues stand about six feet (1.8 m) tall.

TERRA-COTTA ARMY

Qin Shi Huang, the first emperor of China, ordered the creation of an army of life-size clay soldiers that would guard his tomb and protect him in the afterlife. None of the 8,000 statues look the same. Each one is unique.

SOME CHINESE RULERS WORE HATS WITH DANGLING BEADS.

DYNASTIES

China was once led by lines of rulers called dynasties. Power was passed down within the same ruling family, sometimes for a very long time. The longest dynasty lasted more than 200 years.

THE GREAT WALL

China was once divided into many states. Some of the states had their own walls. The first emperor united the country and ordered the walls to be connected. The Great Wall is thousands of miles long. You can still walk on it!

PAPER

A Chinese man named Cai Lun is said to have invented paper. He mashed up wet rags, grass, and wood chips. Then he dried this mixture into sheets of paper.

DID YOU KNOW?

Before paper was invented, ancient Chinese people wrote on bamboo, turtle shells, silk, and bones.

SILK ROAD

The Silk Road wasn't just one road. Traders traveled many roads between China and Europe to buy and sell everything from silk and spices to tea and textiles. These trade routes also helped ideas spread across different areas of the world.

In ancient China, the **dragon** was a symbol of the emperor. Today, it represents **good luck** and **courage.**

ANCIENT GREECE

The Greek Empire once spread across parts of Europe, Africa, and Asia. We have the ancient Greeks to thank for many things, from theater to the Olympic Games!

PARTHENON

TEMPLES

Many ancient Greek buildings still stand. The construction of buildings like this one followed specific rules to ensure that they were strong. The Greek style of architecture is still used in buildings today.

ZEUS

MYTHOLOGY

Ancient Greeks told many adventure tales, or myths, about gods, goddesses, heroes, and monsters. Zeus was the king of the Greek gods. The gods were said to live on Mount Olympus, the highest mountain in Greece.

THEATER

Plays were very popular in ancient Greece. All the actors were men, though some played women's roles. They wore masks to show how their characters were feeling.

OLYMPIC GAMES

The first Olympic Games, held in Olympia, Greece, in 776 B.C., were part of a festival to honor Zeus. In early games, athletes competed in just a few events, including foot races, wrestling, and discus throwing.

ANCIENT ROME

Ancient Rome was once a small village on the Tiber River. It grew into a huge empire that spanned much of what is now Europe, northern Africa, and western Asia.

ART

Romans decorated their homes and public buildings with paintings and sculptures. Floors and walls were often covered in mosaics, designs made from small pieces of tile or stone.

The floor of the Colosseum could be flooded with water for ship battles.

COLOSSEUM

Chariot races and other events were held in this giant theater in the city of Rome.

AQUEDUCTS

The Romans used strong stone arches to make bridges and aqueducts. An aqueduct is a large pipe or channel that carries water a long way. Some ancient Roman aqueducts can still be seen today.

NEW NAMES, SAME GODS

Ancient Romans believed in many of the same gods as the ancient Greeks, but they gave them different names. For example, the Romans' god of the sea was called Neptune, and the Greeks' was called Poseidon.

NEPTUNE

191

THE INCA

Hundreds of years ago, this was the largest empire in what is now Central and South America. Many roads connected Inca cities over thousands of miles.

MACHU PICCHU

This Inca city was built in the Andes Mountains of Peru. It has more than 200 stone buildings.

Llamas can carry a load as heavy as 120 pounds (54 kg).

LLAMAS

These relatives of the camel carried supplies and gave the Inca wool and meat. Llama poop made good fuel for fires!

BUILDING

The Inca carved stone bricks so carefully that their walls stood without anything holding the stones together.

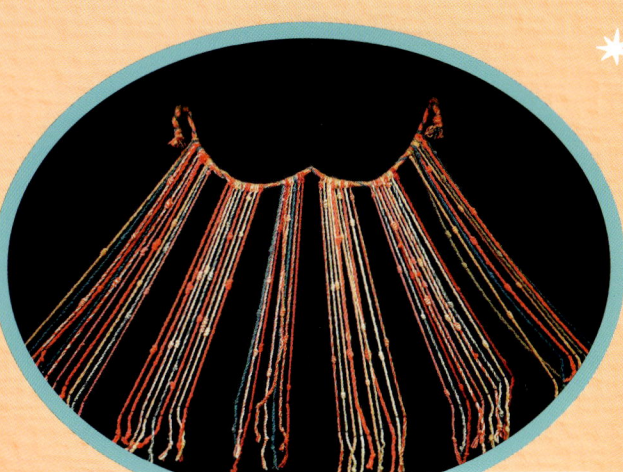

BRIDGES

To cross from one high place to another, the Inca built long bridges out of rope they made from grasses. One of these bridges is still used today—people replace the rope every year!

GOLD SCULPTURE OF A WOMAN

QUIPU

Instead of writing, the Inca tied different colored strings with knots. The color and length of the strings, along with the number and placement of the knots, created different meanings.

SILVER CUP

GOLD SCULPTURE OF AN ANIMAL

GOLD

The Inca created beautiful pieces of jewelry and art from gold and silver. Even the walls in some Inca buildings were covered in these precious metals.

NATIVE NORTH AMERICANS

Many different tribal people have lived all over North America for thousands of years. They still do today.

CLIFF DWELLINGS

Long ago, ancient Pueblo people in the American Southwest built shelters into rocky cliffs using bricks made from clay, straw, and water.

FEATHERS

In the Rosebud Sioux tribe, family and community members may give someone an eagle feather to celebrate a life event.

BEADS

Beading was a type of early Native American artwork. Different tribes developed their own beadwork styles. They wove colorful patterns and designs into clothing and jewelry.

Black, red, white, and blue-green are the colors most often used on totem poles.

POWWOWS

A powwow is a celebration in which Native peoples dance, eat, and sing. These dancers at the Oglala Lakota Nation Pow Wow wear outfits with feathers and beads.

ON THE MOVE

For many years, tribal people living in the American Southwest and Plains hunted large animals like buffalo. They ate the meat and used the skins to make clothing and cone-shaped homes called tepees. Tepees were easy to put up, take down, and move.

BASKETS

Native people have been weaving grasses, bark, and roots into baskets for thousands of years. The baskets are used for everything from storing and serving food to carrying things from place to place.

ARCTIC HUNTERS

For thousands of years, Native people in the Arctic have hunted whales. They spear fish and seals through holes in the ice. The animals are used for food, and their skin, furs, fat, and bones are used to make tools, clothing, and shelter.

TOTEM POLES

Native people on the Northwest Coast carve tree trunks with images and symbols that tell a family's story.

195

IN THE PACIFIC

Long before large sailing ships were invented, people made their way from Asia across the Pacific Ocean to Australia. Over thousands of years, other seafaring people settled on islands all over Oceania.

HUGE HEADS

Rapa Nui, also called Easter Island, is home to nearly 900 gigantic stone heads. These heads are called *moai*. They were carved out of volcanic rock long ago.

FIRST AUSTRALIANS

Aboriginal people arrived in Australia about 60,000 years ago, and they still live there today. Aboriginals created some of the first rock art anywhere. They also invented the didgeridoo, one of the world's oldest musical instruments.

DIDGERIDOO

HULA

Hula has been a part of Hawaiian culture for hundreds of years. The dances honor ancient gods and goddesses, and tell stories.

MAUNA LOA

The Hawaiian Islands formed from volcanic eruptions that happened over thousands of years. The lava cooled into new land. Many Native Hawaiians believe that Pele, the goddess of volcanoes and fire, formed the islands. Eruptions are proof of her power!

SETTING SAIL

The first settlers in the Hawaiian Islands came from islands thousands of miles away. They traveled in large, sturdy canoes. Some of these boats were big enough to hold 80 people!

MEETING PLACE

The Maori people of New Zealand call the country Aotearoa. That means "Land of the Long White Cloud." Maori people gather at special carved houses for meetings, celebrations, and other events.

THAT'S COOL!

WONDERS OF THE WORLD

UFFINGTON WHITE HORSE
This figure of a horse was carved into a hillside in England 3,000 years ago.

PYRAMID OF KUKULKAN
This temple in Mexico has 365 steps, one for each day of the Maya calendar.

ANGKOR WAT
This Buddhist temple in Cambodia is the world's largest religious monument.

PETRA
This city in Jordan was carved into sandstone cliff walls.

NASCA LINES
How ancient people carved these giant pictures in the desert in Peru is still a mystery.

TEMPLE OF KARNAK
Ancient Egyptians began building this temple city more than 3,000 years ago.

PERSEPOLIS
Palaces in this ancient Persian city in Iran were filled with sculptures of warriors and guards.

CHAPTER 8

Bright Ideas

Have you ever had a **SUPERCOOL IDEA?** Made up a **new story** or created a **unique piece** of art? Creative ideas and **inventions** change the way **we live.** **Thinking** big can also make life **more fun!**

201

MIGHTY MACHINES

The first machines ever invented may look simple, but they made it easier for people to do things like get their food, move heavy loads, and more. Many of the machines we use today are based on these early inventions.

PULLEY

PULLEY

A pulley has a wheel with a rope running over it. When you pull down on one end of the rope, it lifts the object attached to the other end. Flagpoles and cranes use pulleys.

Tower cranes use pulley systems to lift heavy loads.

LEVER

LEVER

A lever is a bar or a rod used to lift something. When you push down on the long end of the lever, it lifts the load at the other end. Crowbars, claw hammers, and seesaws are levers.

INCLINED PLANE

A ramp is an inclined plane. Pushing something up a ramp is easier than lifting it straight up. Ancient Egyptians used ramps to build temples and pyramids.

INCLINED PLANES CAN HELP PEOPLE GET AROUND EASIER.

INCLINED PLANE

A slide is an **inclined plane** you can **zoom** down!

WEDGE

When you put two inclined planes back-to-back, you get a wedge. Axes, knives, and plows are wedges.

WEDGE

SCREW

A screw is a circular inclined plane. It's easier to twist a screw into an object than to push it. Screws are used for jar lids, swivel chairs, and water faucets.

DID YOU KNOW?

Escalators, tractors, dishwashers, and other complicated machines are made of many simple machines all working together.

SCREW

Wheel and Axle

A wheel and axle is a machine that turns in a circle. The axle is a rod connected to the center of the wheel. When the axle turns, so does the wheel. Wagons, bikes, and cars all have wheels and axles.

AXLE

WHEEL

SCIENCE ROCKS!

Are you curious about the world? Do you ask a lot of questions? Then you're thinking like a scientist! Science is a special way of learning about the world. Here are just a few kinds of science.

CHEMISTRY

Chemistry studies what matter is made of and how it can change. Matter is anything that takes up space. Everything in the world is made of matter. Even air!

BIOLOGY

Biology is the science of living things. That includes plants and animals—which means people, too! Zoology is the science of animals, and botany is the science of plants. Both are branches of biology.

PHYSICS

Physics is the science of matter and forces, and the ways they work together. Forces make things move. A force is a push or a pull. When you bounce a ball, force is at work.

GEOLOGY

Geology is the science of Earth. Geologists study Earth's surface and deep inside our planet, too.

ASTRONOMY

Planets, stars, galaxies, and space travel are all part of astronomy, the science of space.

ANTHROPOLOGY

How did people live 2,000 years ago? 500 years ago? How do people live today? Anthropology is the study of human societies and cultures and how they change over time.

OCEANOGRAPHY

Oceanographers study how the ocean works, how we can take care of it, and all the plants and animals that live in it.

ENGINEERING

Engineers use what they know about science to design and build new things and to make existing things better. Cars, phones, bridges, and computers are all brought to us by engineers.

POWER ON!

How do you read a book when it's dark outside? Electricity. Now that's a bright idea! But electricity has to travel a long way to get to your home.

1 POWER PLANT

Electricity is made here. Power plants can use solar energy, nuclear energy, wind, water, coal, or natural gas to generate electricity.

2 TRANSMISSION LINES

The electricity travels through thick, tough wires called transmission lines.

3 SUBSTATION

The electricity arrives at smaller buildings called substations. Here the electricity is divided into smaller amounts.

4 POWER LINES

From the substation, electricity travels through smaller lines above or below the ground to your neighborhood—and your house!

5 SERVICE PANEL

At your home, electricity goes into a panel that's connected to a lot of wires.

6 WIRES

From the service panel, the electricity goes through wires in your walls to outlets and switches all over your house. When you turn on your lamp, the lightbulb uses the energy in electricity to create light.

Electricity isn't just for **lights.** It also powers our **refrigerators,** fans, toasters, **air conditioners,** and more.

Where Does Electricity Come From?

We can get electricity from renewable or nonrenewable resources.

RENEWABLE RESOURCES

Energy from the sun and from the movement of water and wind does not run out.

WIND
A wind turbine turns the wind's movement into electricity.

WATER
Dams use rushing water to turn a motor that makes electricity.

SOLAR
Panels that collect sunlight can turn the sun's energy into electricity.

NONRENEWABLE RESOURCES

Coal and natural gas are fuels found deep underground. They are burned to create heat that then helps make electricity. There is not an endless supply of these fuels, so they will run out someday.

COAL
Miners use large machines to dig out coal, then load it into carts.

EVERYDAY INVENTIONS

Some of the things we use every day were once a brand-new idea!

EYEGLASSES

The ancient Romans knew that peering through curved glass could make things look bigger. Around 1284, an Italian inventor put small disks of glass into a frame that could rest on the nose. He made the first pair of glasses!

POPSICLE

In 1905, 11-year-old Frank Epperson accidentally invented this sweet treat. He left a cup of soda with a stick in it on his porch, where it froze overnight.

SNEAKERS

The first rubber-soled athletic shoes were made in the 1860s. About 100 years later, Bill Bowerman put rubber in a waffle iron to create soles that gripped the ground.

ZIPPER

The zipper that closes your backpack or your favorite pair of jeans was invented in 1913. Gideon Sundback designed two rows of "teeth" that lock together with a slider.

ELEVATOR

In 1853, Elisha Otis designed a way to move heavy things up and down in a large building. His elevators—and the brakes that keep them from falling—made another invention possible. Skyscrapers!

POPCORN

What happened when Aztec people heated corn kernels over the fire? Popcorn was born!

MONEY

All kinds of things have been used as money: stones, shells, rice, and cocoa beans, to name a few! Both metal coins and paper money were first used in ancient China.

SLICED BREAD

People have been eating bread for thousands of years, but it wasn't until 1928 that Otto Rohwedder invented a machine that cut bread into sliced loaves.

COMMUNICATION INNOVATION

For thousands of years, it took a long time for news to travel very far. But once inventors started using electricity, communication around the world got a LOT quicker!

HAND TO HAND

Long ago, messages could only travel as fast as a person, horse, or ship could take them.

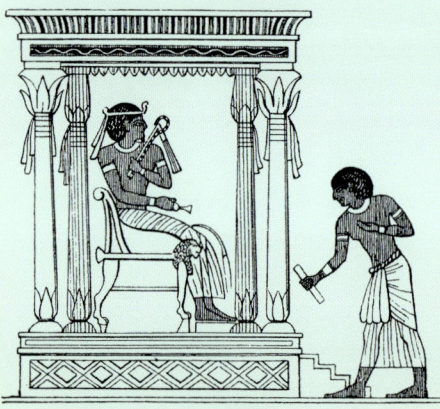

Can you **write your name in Morse code?** Try tapping it out! **Dots** get short taps, **dashes** get long taps.

A TELEGRAPH OPERATOR SENDS A MESSAGE.

ELECTRIC TELEGRAPH

The telegraph was the first machine ever to deliver news in just minutes! It sent messages along a wire using a code of electronic dots and dashes, called Morse code.

TELEPHONE

When you talk into a telephone, it changes your speech into electrical signals. These signals are changed back into sounds by the phone at the other end. The first phones were big! They sent signals through wires.

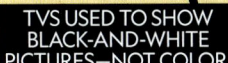

TVS USED TO SHOW BLACK-AND-WHITE PICTURES—NOT COLOR!

TELEVISION

TVs turn electrical signals or radio waves into the action and sounds we see and hear.

COMPUTER

A computer is an electric machine that can be programmed to do a certain job—or many jobs. Early computers were so big they filled a room!

INTERNET

The internet is a network that connects computers around the world. News travels super fast on the internet!

CELL PHONE

Cell phones send and receive calls using radio waves instead of electrical wires. The first cell phone weighed as much as a quart of milk!

SMARTPHONE

Today's smartphones fit in your hand. They are cell phones and computers rolled into one!

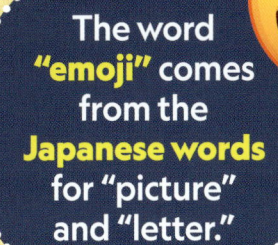
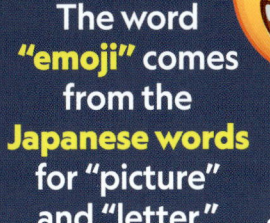

The word **"emoji"** comes from the **Japanese words** for "picture" and "letter."

WRITING AND BOOKS

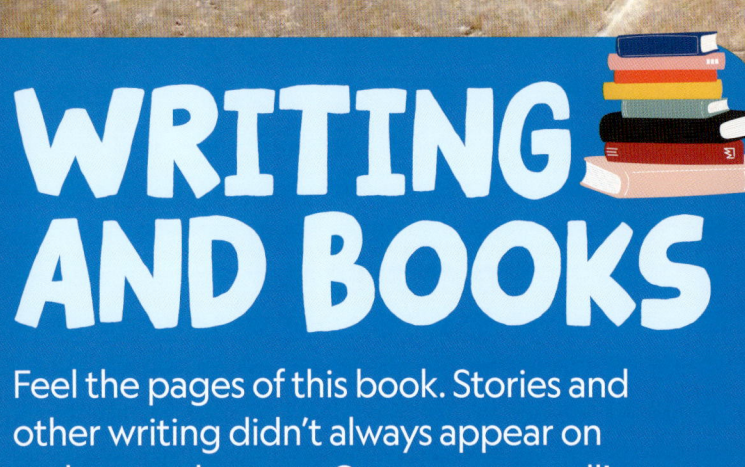

Feel the pages of this book. Stories and other writing didn't always appear on such smooth paper. Or on paper at all!

CUNEIFORM

The earliest form of writing was made by pressing a tool into wet clay. Cuneiform was developed about 5,000 years ago in what is now Iraq.

EARLY BOOKS

Ancient Chinese books were made of bamboo pieces, called slips, tied together. Each slip contained a column of characters.

PICTURES

Ancient Maya writing looked like art: 800 pictures stood for sounds and ideas. These pictures were called hieroglyphs.

CODEX

The Aztec people of Mexico used pictures and symbols to write on deerskin or tree bark, which was folded into panels called a codex.

Before printing was **invented**, books had to be **copied** by hand.

MOVABLE TYPE

The first movable type was made with clay blocks almost 1,000 years ago in China. There was one character on each block. The blocks could be rearranged to form different words.

FIRST PRINTING PRESS

PRINTING PRESS

In Germany in 1440, Johannes Gutenberg built a machine called a press that could print pages quickly using movable metal type. Today, books are printed all over the world using computer technology.

ALL KINDS OF ART

Art is something people create for others to look at, listen to, read, or experience. There are so many ways to make beautiful art!

DRAWING

With a pencil, crayon, charcoal, or ink, an artist can create an image using just a few strokes.

COLLAGE

A collage is made by gluing things to a surface. You can make a collage from all sorts of things, from paper and buttons to leaves, shells, and more.

FABRIC ART

Quilting is a way of sewing pieces of fabric together to make a picture or design.

MOSAIC

This kind of art is like a jigsaw puzzle! A mosaic is a picture that is made by fitting together small pieces of stone, pottery, glass, tile, or paper.

PAINTING

Painters use brushes and other tools to apply paint to a canvas, paper, or another surface.

SCULPTURE

Sculptures can be made out of almost anything—wood, stone, clay, glass, plastic, even recycled trash!

PHOTOGRAPHY

Cameras can capture a scene from real life and turn it into art.

MUSIC

Music is an art we can hear. Human voices and instruments make music. It has melodies, patterns, and rhythms.

SING IT

You have a built-in instrument—your voice! With your voice and your mouth, you can sing, hum, and whistle!

READING MUSIC

Musical notation is a way to write down music. Musicians can read these notes. The notes tell them how to play a song even if they have never heard it before.

PLAY IT

When you blow into a trumpet, tuba, or trombone, air moves through the instrument to make music.

Whales **sing,** too! Their songs can travel **thousands of miles** in the **water.**

DANCE

Tap your toes, wave your arms, and move to the beat of the music. Let's dance!

CEREMONIAL DANCE

These special dances often celebrate a culture's history. Sometimes the dancers' movements imitate the movement of an animal or something else in nature.

BALLET

Ballet dancers leap and turn in the air. A few other kinds of dance are salsa, jazz, and hip-hop.

EVERYBODY DANCE!

Dancing is fun! You can dance with friends on the playground or at a party—or all by yourself!

MOVE YOUR BODY

You can use your whole body to dance! You can hop, sway, jump, twist, and shake to the rhythm of the music.

Male **blue-footed boobies** dance to show off their blue feet to **females.**

TAMBOURINE

PIANO

SITAR

MUSICAL INSTRUMENTS

People have been creating and playing musical instruments for thousands of years. Here are just a few of the instruments that people play around the globe today.

DJEMBE

MARIMBA

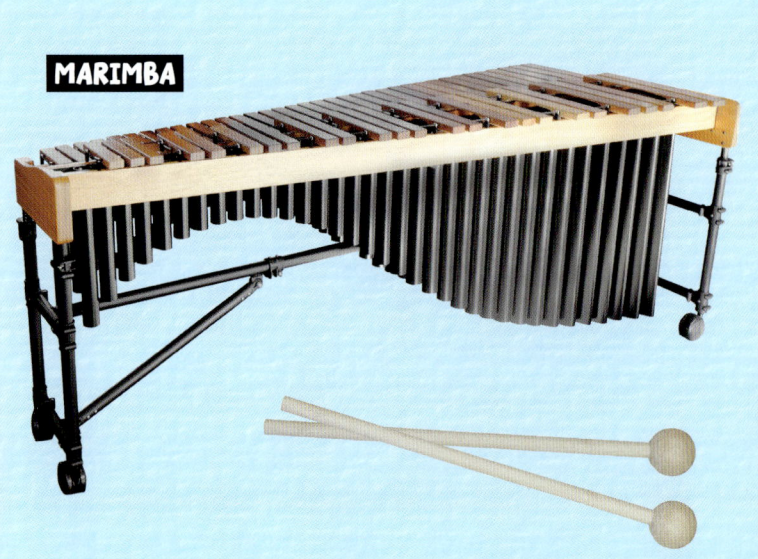

GONG

FLUTE

XYLOPHONE

TRUMPET

DIDGERIDOO

ELECTRIC GUITAR

VIOLIN

219

THAT'S COOL!

SUPER STRUCTURES

TALLEST FERRIS WHEEL:
AIN DUBAI, DUBAI, UNITED ARAB EMIRATES

LARGEST INDOOR WATER PARK:
TROPICAL ISLANDS, KRAUSNICK, GERMANY

LARGEST SWIMMING POOL:
SAN ALFONSO DEL MAR, ALGARROBO, CHILE

BIGGEST HOUSE:
ISTANA NURUL IMAN,
BANDAR SERI
BEGAWAN, BRUNEI

TALLEST BUILDING:
BURJ KHALIFA, DUBAI,
UNITED ARAB EMIRATES

BIGGEST SPORTS STADIUM:
RUNGRADO 1ST OF MAY STADIUM,
PYONGYANG, NORTH KOREA

HIGHEST BRIDGE:
BEIPANJIANG
BRIDGE, CHINA

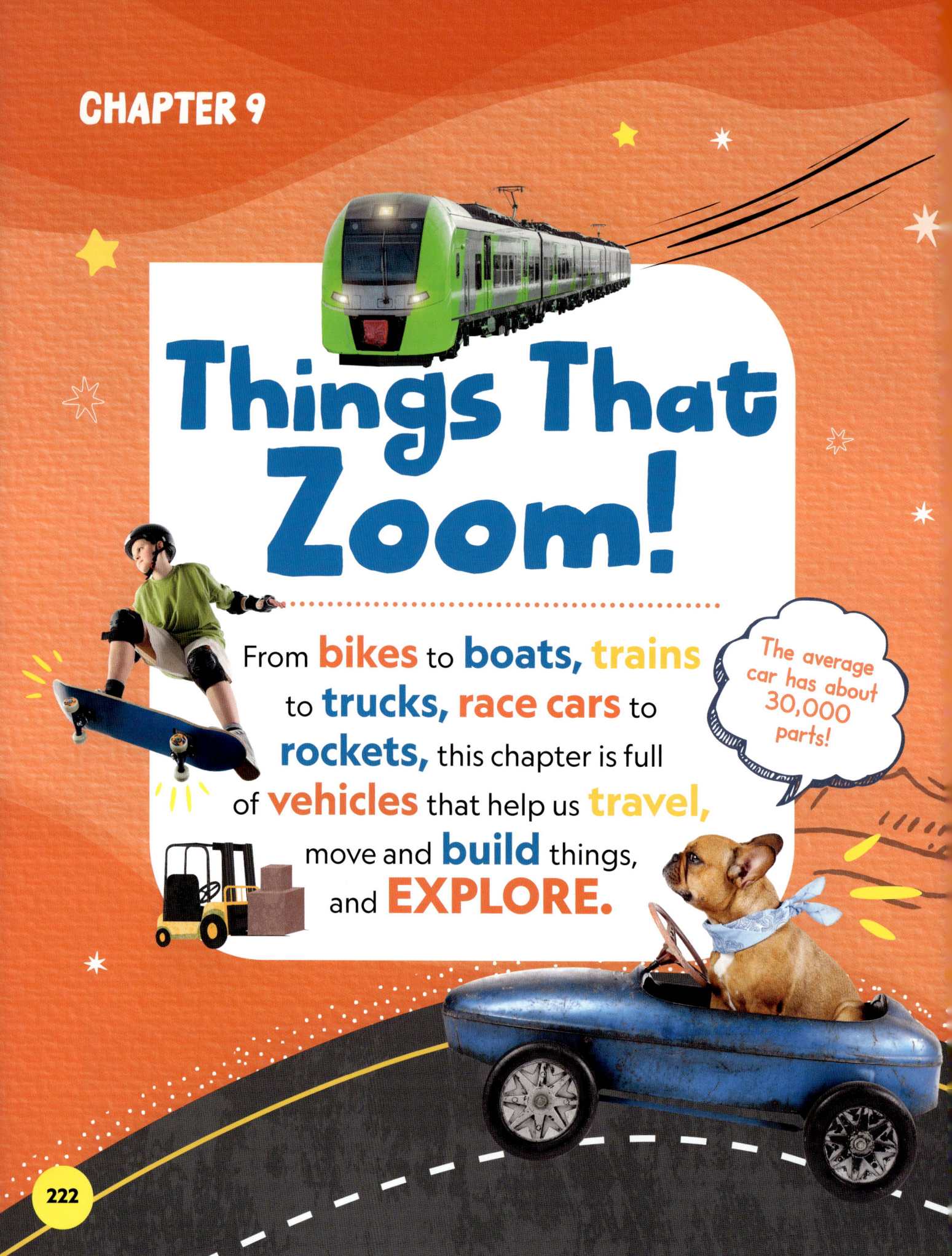

CHAPTER 9

Things That Zoom!

From **bikes** to **boats, trains** to **trucks, race cars** to **rockets,** this chapter is full of **vehicles** that help us **travel,** move and **build** things, and **EXPLORE.**

The average car has about 30,000 parts!

IT'S HOW WE ROLL

Did you know that the oldest wheels had nothing to do with going places? They were for making pottery. But about 5,000 years ago, someone turned a wheel on its side, and humans were on a roll!

WHEELBARROWS

Add handles and a wheel to a box, and you've got a simple cart that can help you carry heavy things. Wheelbarrows were some of the earliest vehicles on wheels.

Racing chariots were small and light so that they could move as fast as possible.

CHARIOTS

In ancient times, horses pulled these two-wheeled carts in races, battles, and special ceremonies.

CARRIAGES AND WAGONS

Four wheels made a vehicle more stable—and heavier. The bigger wagons got, the more they could carry, and the more horses or oxen it took to pull them.

EARLY CARS

The first cars looked a lot like horse-drawn carriages—just without the horse! Instead of being pulled by animals, an engine pushed them forward.

CRAZY FOR CARS

Over the years, cars have been made in many different shapes and sizes. Today's cars are much faster, quieter, easier to control, and safer than early cars.

WHAT MAKES A CAR GO?

Many cars, trucks, and other vehicles are powered by machines called engines. Engines turn energy into movement.

OIL

Some cars and trucks are powered by gasoline, a liquid fuel made from oil. Gasoline burns inside the car's engine, creating bursts of energy that make the car go.

ELECTRICITY

Electric cars are powered by electricity stored in batteries. When the batteries run low on power, you plug them into an outlet to recharge them.

HYBRID

Some vehicles, called hybrids, run on both gasoline and battery power.

TRICYCLE

POGO STICK

PEOPLE POWER!

Some things that go need energy from people. Slide on skis, glide on skates, and speed by with bikes! Which ones have you tried?

SKATEBOARD

ROLLER SKATES

SCOOTER

BICYCLES

SKIS

Unicycles don't have handlebars! To turn, a rider leans in the direction they want to go.

SURFBOARD

UNICYCLE

227

TRAINS

Choo choo! Trains can move a lot of people—or stuff—all at once. Trains run on a schedule, so you can pick which time works for you. All aboard!

STEAM MACHINES

The first trains were called iron horses. They were powered by engines that made steam by burning coal or wood to heat water.

The **shape** of a **high-speed train's nose** helps it **move faster.**

HIGH-SPEED TRAINS

High-speed passenger trains can zoom along at up to 285 miles an hour (460 km/h). *Whoosh!*

FREIGHT TRAINS

These powerful trains haul large loads such as wood and building materials. Some boxcars are refrigerated for shipping cold food. The longest freight trains can have hundreds of boxcars!

PASSENGER TRAINS

Passenger trains can carry a lot of people. Some of them even have beds where you can sleep on overnight trips!

SUBWAY TRAINS

Underground subway trains move below a city's streets and buildings. The first subway opened in London, England, in 1863. They are often the fastest way to get around a city. No traffic jams here!

STREETCARS

A streetcar is a vehicle that runs on tracks laid on a city street. They drive alongside cars. Most streetcars run on electricity.

CONSTRUCTION SITE

You'll find some of the most gigantic things that go at construction sites. These huge vehicles dig, move, and lift dirt and rocks to build roads, bridges, and buildings.

Construction workers use safety helmets called **hard hats** to protect their **heads.**

A **cement truck** mixes and pours cement for foundations, driveways, sidewalks, and more.

A **compactor** smooths out pavement to make roads.

A **crane** lifts heavy materials up high.

An **excavator** has a shovel that digs and scoops out dirt and rocks.

Safety goggles **protect** your eyes from **dust** and **dirt.**

A bulldozer moves piles of dirt and rocks.

A dump truck hauls loads of rocks or dirt to or from a construction site.

A front loader scoops and moves dirt and rocks.

A forklift carries and delivers building supplies.

231

IN THE WATER

When it's time to float, you need a boat! People have traveled by boat on lakes, rivers, and oceans for thousands of years.

A sailboat usually has **two sails:** a **mainsail** and a **headsail.**

SAILBOAT

Wind power makes this boat move. When its sails catch the breeze, the boat moves forward.

CANOE

One or two people can paddle a canoe. The faster you paddle, the faster you'll go!

SUBMARINE

Submarines are ships that can travel underwater or on the water's surface.

AIRCRAFT CARRIER

This ship has a large deck where planes can take off and land.

SPEEDBOAT

These boats have powerful motors that make them move fast.

CONTAINER SHIP

These huge ships carry cargo—everything from cars to computers—across the seas from one country to another.

UP, UP, AND AWAY!

People have invented many different ways to lift off from Earth. Now we can fly to almost any place on our planet—and even to places far beyond it!

JET POWER

Jet engines mix air with fuel to create a blast of gas that pushes the plane forward. The biggest jets can carry up to 850 passengers!

In 1783, the **first hot-air balloon** lifted off. Its **passengers** included a sheep, a **rooster,** and a **duck.**

EARLY FLIGHT

In 1903, Orville Wright piloted the first successful engine-powered airplane flight at a beach in Kitty Hawk, North Carolina, U.S.A. The plane that he and his brother Wilbur designed was called the *Wright Flyer.*

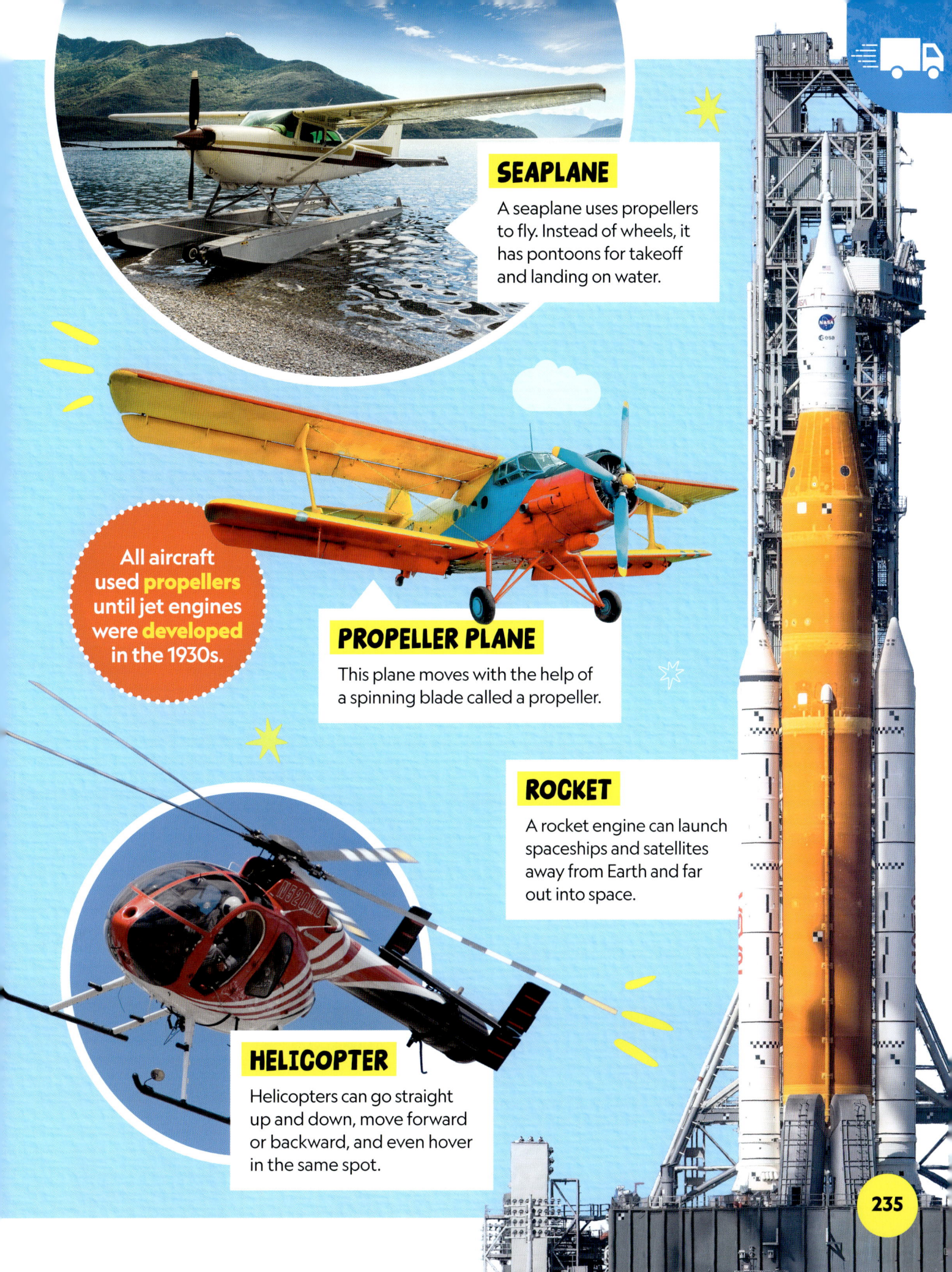

SEAPLANE

A seaplane uses propellers to fly. Instead of wheels, it has pontoons for takeoff and landing on water.

All aircraft used **propellers** until jet engines were **developed** in the 1930s.

PROPELLER PLANE

This plane moves with the help of a spinning blade called a propeller.

ROCKET

A rocket engine can launch spaceships and satellites away from Earth and far out into space.

HELICOPTER

Helicopters can go straight up and down, move forward or backward, and even hover in the same spot.

THAT'S COOL!

RECORD-SETTING VEHICLES

FASTEST TRAIN:
MAGLEV

BIGGEST MONSTER TRUCK:
BIGFOOT 5

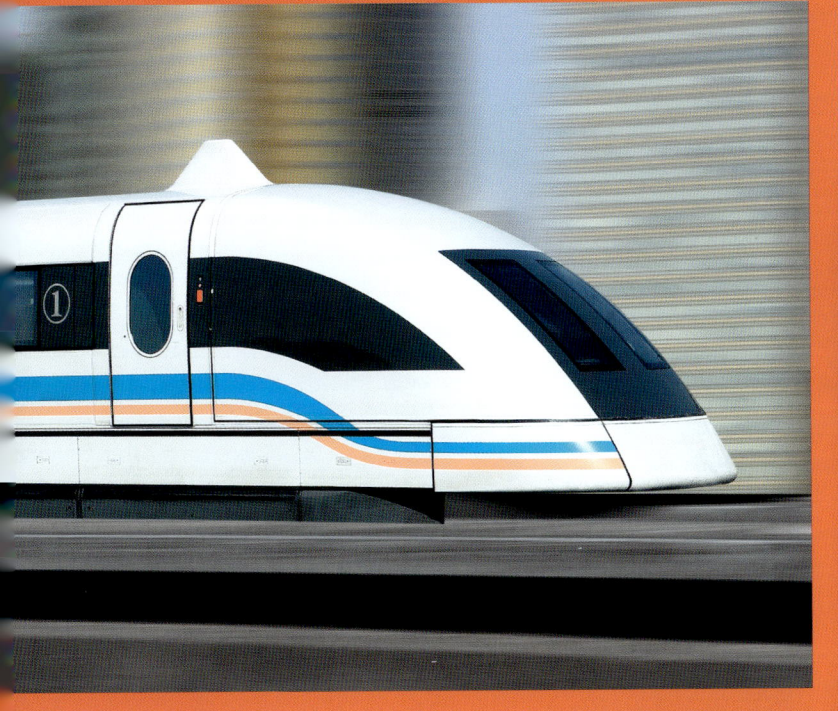

LARGEST AIRPLANE:
STRATOLAUNCH ROC

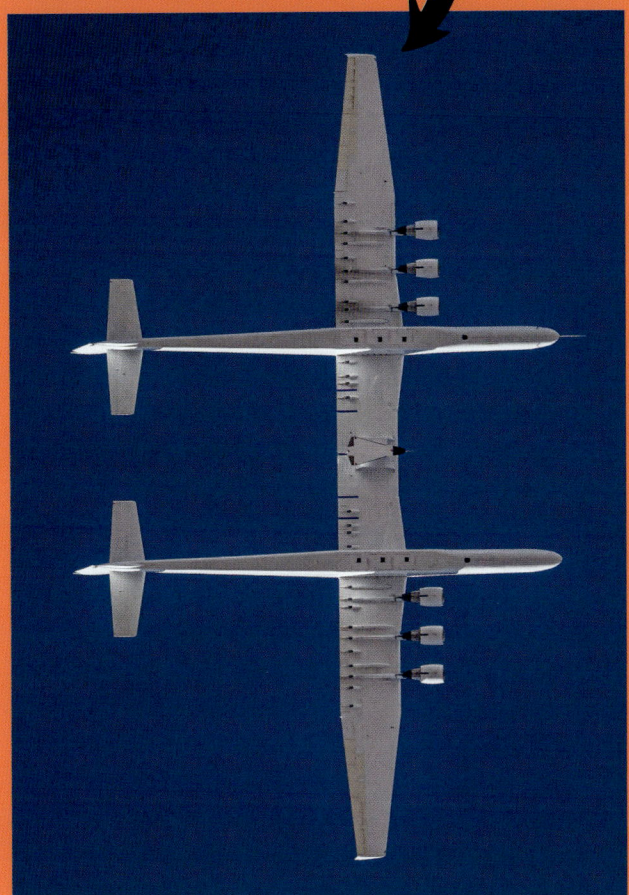

LARGEST CRUISE SHIP:
ICON OF THE SEAS

LARGEST VEHICLE:
BAGGER 293

SMALLEST CAR:
PEEL P50

CHAPTER 10

Out of This World

Blast off into the dark night sky to see stars swirl in galaxies, planets move around the sun, and space rocks spin. Speed along with spacecraft as they explore Earth's neighborhood and beyond.

The universe is about 13 billion years old!

AWESOME ATMOSPHERE

An invisible blanket wraps all around Earth, kind of like the peel around an orange. This blanket that we cannot see is called the atmosphere. It's made of air and it has five different layers.

EXOSPHERE

This is the outer layer of our atmosphere. It gradually fades away into space. There is no air to breathe here.

Air gets **thinner** and more spread out the **higher** you go in the atmosphere.

THERMOSPHERE

This is the hottest layer of Earth's atmosphere. It absorbs a lot of energy from the sun.

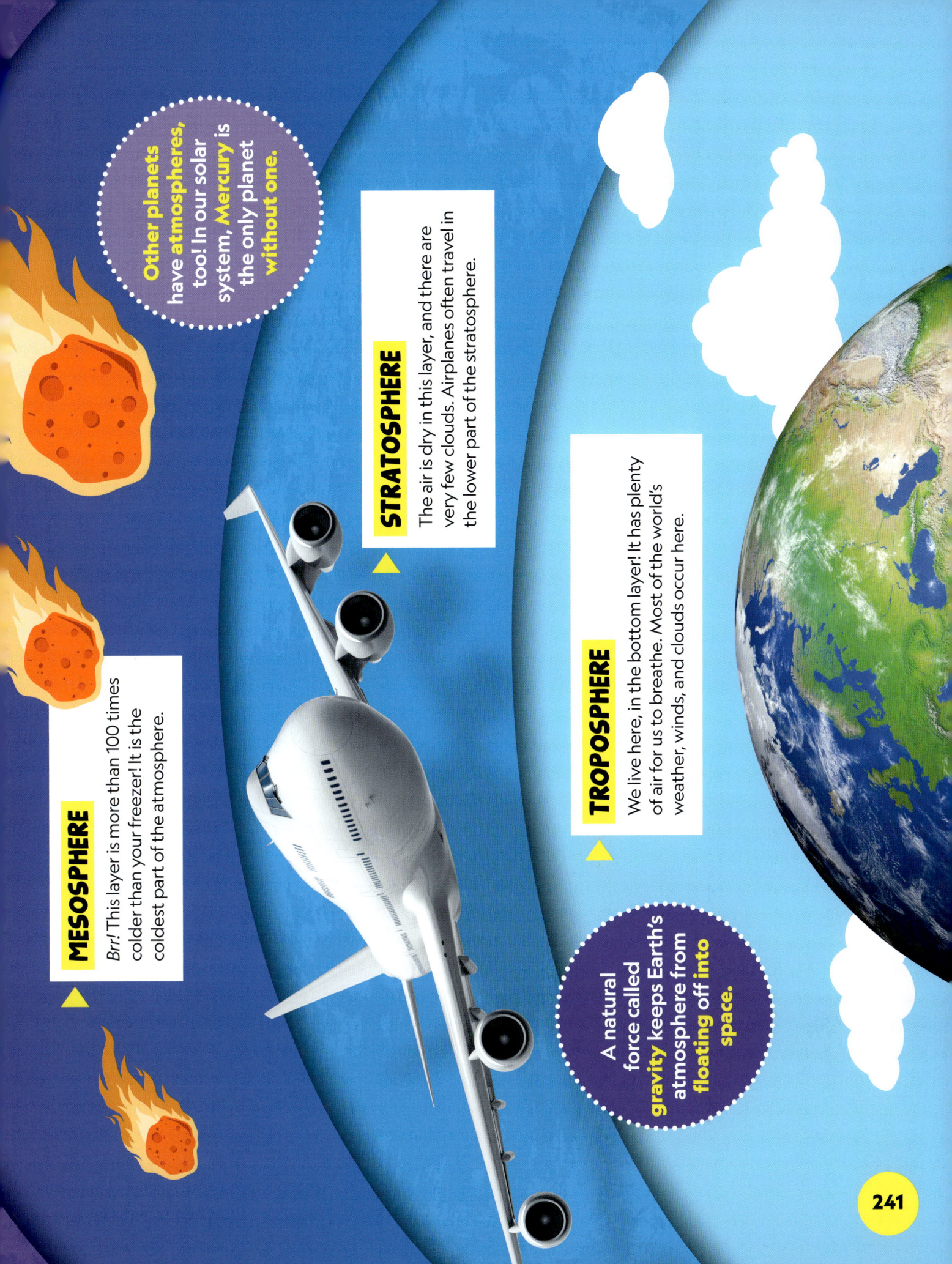

Other planets have atmospheres, too! In our solar system, **Mercury** is the only planet **without one.**

STRATOSPHERE

The air is dry in this layer, and there are very few clouds. Airplanes often travel in the lower part of the stratosphere.

TROPOSPHERE

We live here, in the bottom layer! It has plenty of air for us to breathe. Most of the world's weather, winds, and clouds occur here.

MESOSPHERE

Brr! This layer is more than 100 times colder than your freezer! It is the coldest part of the atmosphere.

A natural force called **gravity** keeps Earth's atmosphere from **floating off into space.**

OUR SOLAR SYSTEM

The sun is at the center of Earth's solar system. Eight planets travel around this big star in a path called an orbit.

MARS

This dusty desert world is also called the red planet. The color of Mars comes from the large amount of rust in its dirt and rocks.

MERCURY

This is the smallest planet and the one closest to the sun. It orbits the sun faster than any other planet.

SUN

The sun is huge! More than a million Earths could fit inside it.

VENUS

Clouds swirl above this hot planet's surface. Venus has a lot of active volcanoes.

JUPITER

This is the biggest planet in our solar system. Its Great Red Spot is a storm that has been swirling for about 150 years!

URANUS

Water and gases surround this icy planet's rocky core. The clouds on its blue surface smell like rotten eggs!

NEPTUNE

The farthest planet from the sun is dark, cold, and windy.

GREAT RED SPOT

SATURN

The large rings that circle this gas giant are made of ice. Some ice pieces are the size of a speck of dust. Other ice pieces are as big as a house!

EARTH

Earth is the only planet in our solar system that has liquid water on its surface. As far as we know, it's also the only planet that has living things.

DID YOU KNOW?

This picture doesn't exactly show how big each planet is compared to the others, or how far apart they really are. Neptune is so far away from Earth that the only spacecraft to have ever reached it took 12 years to get there!

EARTH'S SUN

The sun is a star—and not just any star. As Earth orbits the sun, this star gives the plants and animals on our planet warmth and light.

BIG BALL OF FIRE

Earth's sun is an enormous spinning ball of superhot gas.

HOT STUFF

A day that's 100°F (38°C) on Earth seems really hot. But the sun is 10,000°F (5538°C) at its surface and 27 million°F (15 million°C) at its core!

The **sun** is about **93 million miles** (150 million km) from **Earth**.

If you could drive a car to the sun, it would take about 176 years!

SUNSPOTS

These dark spots on the sun's surface are areas that are cooler than the rest.

SOLAR FLARES

A sunspot can cause a huge explosion, called a solar flare, on the sun's surface.

EARTH'S MOON

The moon orbits Earth. It is rocky and cold. It takes about 27 days for the moon to complete its orbit around Earth.

NEAR AND FAR

We can only see one side of the moon from Earth. The side we see is called the near side. The side that faces away from Earth is called the far side.

CRATERS

Space rocks called meteoroids hit the moon millions of years ago and left dents, or craters, all over the surface. You can see craters when you look up at the moon!

The **moon** is about **240,000 miles** (386,000 km) from **Earth.**

If you could drive a car to the moon, it would take about six months!

Phases of the Moon

The moon is a dark place, but it looks bright when the sun's light bounces off its surface. As the moon orbits Earth, the amount of that light we see changes and the shape we can see changes, too. These changes are called the phases of the moon.

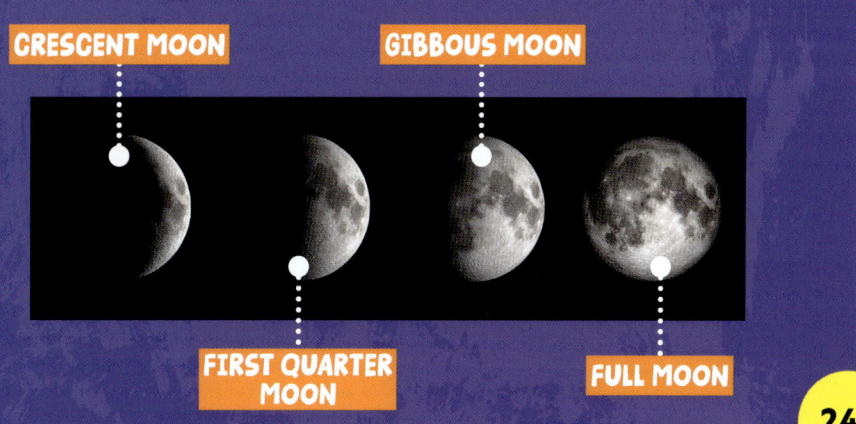

CRESCENT MOON

GIBBOUS MOON

FIRST QUARTER MOON

FULL MOON

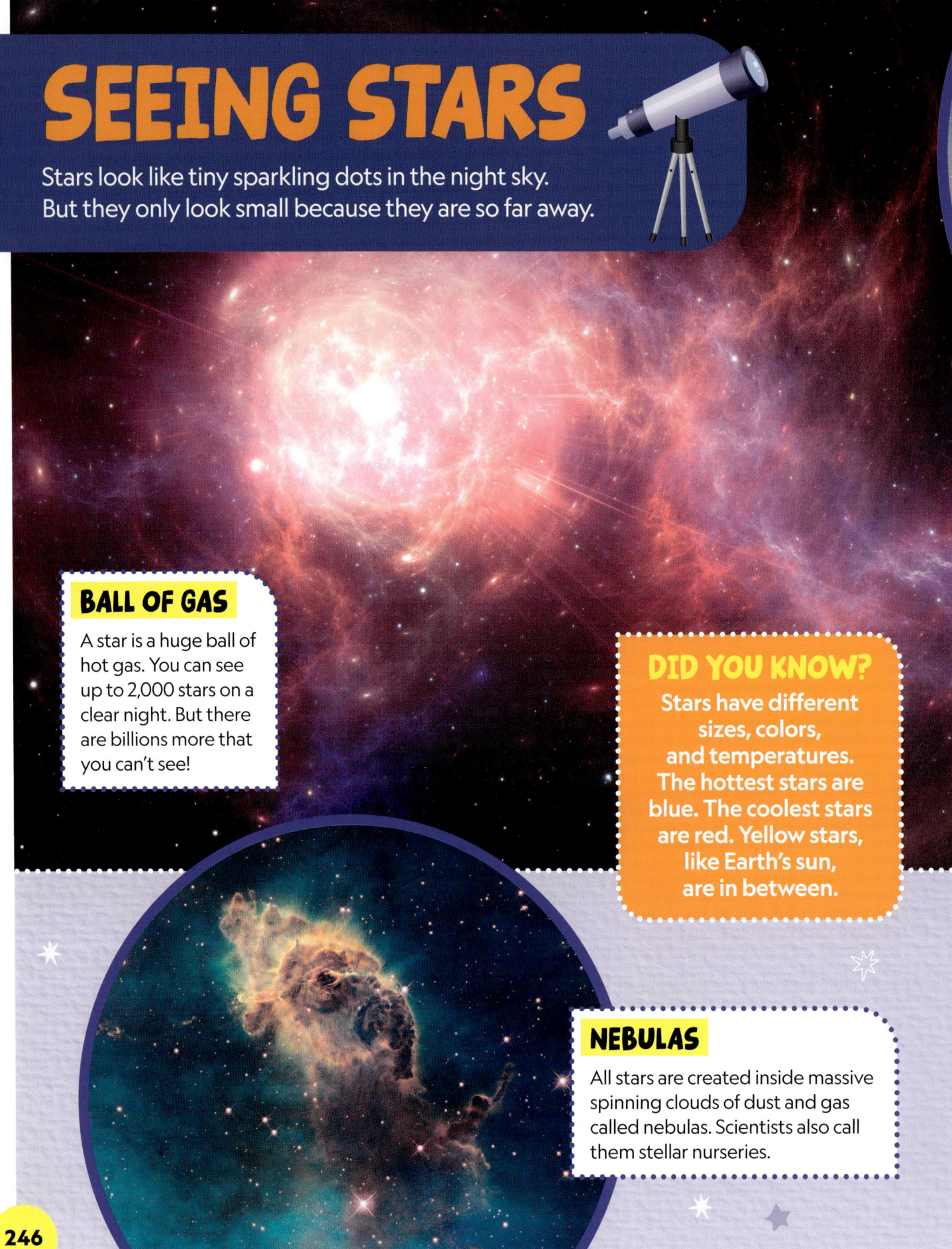

SEEING STARS

Stars look like tiny sparkling dots in the night sky. But they only look small because they are so far away.

BALL OF GAS

A star is a huge ball of hot gas. You can see up to 2,000 stars on a clear night. But there are billions more that you can't see!

DID YOU KNOW?

Stars have different sizes, colors, and temperatures. The hottest stars are blue. The coolest stars are red. Yellow stars, like Earth's sun, are in between.

NEBULAS

All stars are created inside massive spinning clouds of dust and gas called nebulas. Scientists also call them stellar nurseries.

MILKY WAY

Galaxy Shapes

Galaxies have different shapes. The three main kinds are spiral, irregular, and elliptical. Spiral galaxies, like the Milky Way, are shaped like a pinwheel. Irregular galaxies do not have a particular shape. Elliptical galaxies are shaped like an egg.

SPIRAL

ELLIPTICAL

IRREGULAR

GALAXY

A galaxy is a group of stars, gas, and dust held together by gravity. There are billions of galaxies in the universe. Our solar system is in a galaxy called the Milky Way.

ORION, THE HUNTER

CONSTELLATIONS

Since ancient times, people have gazed at the stars and imagined shapes called constellations. They used these star shapes to create stories, track the seasons, and find their way.

BIG DIPPER

A ROCKY WORLD

The solar system is also home to millions of asteroids, comets, and meteors. These are fancy names for space rocks!

COMET

Comets are made of rock, dust, and icy gases. When a comet gets close to the sun, the ice begins to melt. That creates a tail behind the comet that we can sometimes see from Earth.

A **meteor** is also called a **shooting star.**

METEOR

Sometimes a small chunk breaks off from a comet or an asteroid. When this space rock comes close to Earth and burns up in the air, it's called a meteor.

KUIPER BELT

KUIPER BELT

This ring of icy objects is beyond Neptune's orbit. Billions of comets and four of the five dwarf planets—Haumea, Eris, Makemake, and Pluto—are found here.

METEORITE

Meteors usually burn up in the air before they reach the ground. But if a meteor reaches Earth's surface, it's called a meteorite.

There are **five dwarf planets** in our solar system. "Dwarf" means small. These planets are **smaller** than the eight big planets.

ASTEROID BELT

A ring of rocks called asteroids orbits the sun between Mars and Jupiter. Ceres, the closest dwarf planet to the sun, is found in the asteroid belt.

BLASTOFF!

There are plenty of ways to explore space—even parts that humans can't reach! Tools like telescopes, probes, and satellites can collect information and send it back to scientists on Earth.

ASTRONAUT

Scientists who work in space are called astronauts. They train for many years to become space explorers.

SATELLITE

What will the weather be today? A satellite can answer that! These machines orbit Earth. They can track weather across the planet, make maps, send television signals, and connect cell phones.

ROCKET

A rocket can deliver a probe, transport astronauts, or launch a satellite into orbit.

INTERNATIONAL SPACE STATION

This spacecraft orbits Earth. Astronauts from around the world travel here to live and work.

At the International Space Station, astronauts hook sleeping bags to the wall so they don't float around in their sleep!

JAMES WEBB SPACE TELESCOPE

This telescope is the length of two school buses! It orbits the sun and takes pictures of faraway galaxies and nebulas.

PROBE

A probe can orbit, fly by, or land on a comet, asteroid, or planet to collect information.

SPACE SUIT

Outside a spacecraft, humans cannot survive in space without a special suit. It protects them and gives them oxygen to breathe.

EXPLORING MARS

Mars is more like Earth than any other planet in the solar system. Because of this, scientists have launched spacecraft and robotic explorers to look for signs of life on the red planet. These high-tech machines continue to gather information so that people can visit—or even live on—Earth's neighbor one day.

LANDERS

This kind of probe lands on a planet and stays in one location. A lander found water deep below the surface of Mars.

DID YOU KNOW?

The Curiosity rover landed on Mars in 2012. It has 17 cameras, a laser, and a drill. It also has a robotic arm that can hold a camera and send photos back to Earth.

ROVERS

Scientists on Earth use a remote control to move a rover around on Mars. A rover can take pictures, record weather, and test rocks and soil.

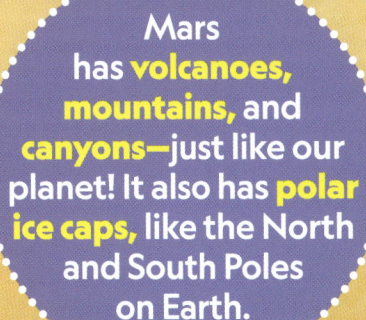

Mars has **volcanoes, mountains,** and **canyons**—just like our planet! It also has **polar ice caps,** like the North and South Poles on Earth.

ORBITERS

Spacecraft are circling Mars to collect information. The NASA orbiter Mars Odyssey took pictures of the planet's entire surface.

TRAVEL TO MARS

Because a round-trip visit to Mars could take almost two years, scientists need to design a spacecraft that can carry enough fuel, oxygen, water, and food.

SIGNS OF LIFE

In addition to water, probes have found a gas called methane. This could be from rocks, but it could also be made by tiny living things called bacteria.

MARS GARDEN

On the International Space Station, astronauts have grown vegetables in soil that was made to copy the dirt on Mars.

HOME SWEET HOME

What would a house on Mars look like? Experts have many ideas about how to keep people safe from the planet's swirling dust storms and cold temperatures.

THAT'S COOL!

SPACE SENSATIONS

BIGGEST VOLCANO
Mars is home to Olympus Mons, the biggest volcano in the solar system.

HOTTEST PLANET
Even though Mercury is closest to the sun, Venus is hotter!

SPACE TOUR
Some companies have started taking tourists into space.

PAC-MAN NEBULA
Nicknamed Pac-Man, this star-forming cloud looks like it is chomping through space.

RAINING DIAMONDS
Scientists think that diamond rain may fall on Neptune and Uranus.

URANUS

GHOSTS
Sometimes it can look like ghostly figures are rising from clouds of gas and dust in space.

COLDEST PLANET
Neptune is the coldest planet.

255

GLOSSARY

AMPHIBIANS a group of cold-blooded animals with backbones; in some species, larval young live in water and breathe through gills

ANTENNAE a pair of long, thin body parts on the heads of most insects

AQUEDUCT a structure used to carry water across long distances

ARACHNIDS a group of animals with no backbones, two body segments, and usually eight legs

ASTEROID a small rocky space object

ASTRONOMY the study of space

ATMOSPHERE the mixture of gases that surround a planet

BIOLOGY the study of living things

BIRDS a group of warm-blooded vertebrate animals that have feathers and wings and hatch from an egg; most can fly

BLUBBER the fat that keeps many ocean mammals warm

CAMOUFLAGE the ability of an animal to blend in with its surroundings

CHEMISTRY the study of substances and the ways they can change

CLIMATE an area's normal weather, measured over a long period of time

CONSTELLATION a grouping of stars that makes an imaginary picture

CONTINENT a large area of land on Earth

DESERT an area that receives very little rainfall

DIET what an animal eats

DIGESTIVE SYSTEM a group of body parts that break down food to make energy

DYNASTY leaders from many generations of the same family

EMPIRE a government that has control of many areas or territories

ENERGY the ability to move and do work

ENGINE a machine that turns energy into movement

ENGINEERING the use of science to design and build things like bridges, machines, and software

EQUATOR an imaginary line that wraps around the center of Earth

EXTINCT no longer in existence; died out

FISH cold-blooded vertebrate animals that live in water and breathe through gills

FLOCK a group of birds that feed and travel together

FOSSIL preserved remains or traces of ancient animals or plants

FUNGUS a living thing that is neither animal nor plant, such as mushrooms

GALAXY a very large group of stars, gas, and dust held together by gravity

GEOLOGY the study of Earth's rocks, minerals, and land

GRAVITY the force that pulls things toward one another

HERD a group of mammals living together

HIEROGLYPHS writing that uses pictures to represent ideas

HOOF a hard, curved horn that protects a mammal's foot

INSECTS a group of small invertebrate animals with three body segments, one pair of antennae, and six legs; some have wings

INVERTEBRATE an animal without a spinal column, or backbone

MAMMALS a group of vertebrate animals that are warm-blooded, breathe air, have hair, and nurse their young

MARSUPIALS a group of mammals whose females generally carry their young in a pouch

MATE one of a pair of animals that have babies together

METAMORPHOSIS a complete change in the form of an animal as it develops into an adult

METEORITE a piece of a meteor that falls to Earth

MIGRATE to move regularly from one place to another

MOON a natural object that orbits a planet

MOSAIC an art form that uses small pieces of colored stone or clay

MUMMY a dead body that has been preserved and wrapped in cloth

MYTHOLOGY a collection of stories about the gods and legends of a particular culture

NATIVE original to a particular place

NEBULA a cloud of stardust from exploded stars

NERVOUS SYSTEM the brain, spinal cord, and all of the nerves in the body

NOCTURNAL active at night

NUTRIENT a substance that living things need to grow

OCEANOGRAPHY the study of oceans and ocean life

ORBIT the path through space around a planet or a star

ORGAN a body part that performs a particular function

PALEONTOLOGY the study of fossils

PHYSICS the study of matter and energy and how they interact

PLANET a large, round object that orbits a star

POLLINATION the transfer of grains of pollen between flowering plants

PREDATOR an animal that eats other animals

PREY an animal that is eaten by other animals

PROBE a device that collects information in space

PTEROSAUR an extinct flying reptile

REPTILES a group of vertebrate animals that are cold-blooded and usually slither or walk on short legs; generally covered with scales or bony plates

RHYTHM the beat or time patterns in music

ROVER a vehicle that explores the surface of a planet or moon

SAP the liquid that moves through a tree or other plant

SATELLITE a spacecraft that orbits a planet and is used for research, communication, tracking weather, and more

SAVANNA an area of grassland with scattered trees

SEASON a period of time in each year with particular weather conditions

SENSES ways of collecting information about the world, including sight, smell, touch, hearing, and taste

SHELTER a place that protects people or animals

SKELETON the structure of bones that supports the body in humans and other vertebrates

SOLAR SYSTEM a star and the objects that orbit it

SPECIES a type or unique kind of animal, plant, or fungus

STAR a bright shining ball of gases such as Earth's sun

TALON a strong curved claw on a large bird

TEMPLE a building meant for worship or prayer

TUNDRA an area of partially frozen ground with few trees

TUSK a long, pointed tooth that sticks out past an animal's mouth

VEHICLE something that moves and carries people and things

VERTEBRATE an animal with a spinal column, or backbone

WEATHER the combined temperature, wind, and water in the air at any particular time and place

FIND OUT MORE

AGES 4 TO 8

Brydon, Alli. *Little Kids First Nature Guide: Bugs*. National Geographic, 2022.

Brydon, Alli. *Little Kids First Nature Guide: Explore the Beach*. National Geographic, 2023.

Buckley, James, Jr. *Little Kids First Big Book of Sports*. National Geographic, 2023.

Carney, Elizabeth. *Little Kids First Big Book of the World*. National Geographic, 2015.

de Seve, Karen. *Little Kids First Big Book of Things That Go*. National Geographic, 2017.

de Seve, Karen. *Little Kids First Big Book of Weather*. National Geographic, 2017.

Donohue, Moira Rose. *Little Kids First Big Book of the Rain Forest*. National Geographic, 2018.

Donohue, Moira Rose. *Little Kids First Big Book of Rocks, Minerals, and Shells*. National Geographic, 2021.

Donohue, Moira Rose. *Little Kids First Nature Guide: Birds*. National Geographic, 2024.

Esbaum, Jill. *Little Kids First Big Book of How*. National Geographic, 2016.

Esbaum, Jill. *Little Kids First Big Book of Where*. National Geographic, 2020.

Esbaum, Jill. *Little Kids First Big Book of Who*. National Geographic, 2015.

Esbaum, Jill. *Little Kids First Big Book of Why 2*. National Geographic, 2018.

Hughes, Catherine D. *Little Kids First Big Book of Animals*. National Geographic, 2010.

Hughes, Catherine D. *Little Kids First Big Book of Birds*. National Geographic, 2016.

Hughes, Catherine D. *Little Kids First Big Book of Bugs*. National Geographic, 2014.

Hughes, Catherine D. *Little Kids First Big Book of Dinosaurs*. National Geographic, 2011.

Hughes, Catherine D. *Little Kids First Big Book of the Ocean*. National Geographic, 2013.

Hughes, Catherine D. *Little Kids First Big Book of Pets*. National Geographic, 2019.

Hughes, Catherine D. *Little Kids First Big Book of Reptiles and Amphibians*. National Geographic, 2020.

Hughes, Catherine D. *Little Kids First Big Book of Space*. National Geographic, 2012.

Myers, Maya. *Little Kids First Big Book of Baby Animals*. National Geographic, 2022.

Shields, Amy. *Little Kids First Big Book of Why*. National Geographic, 2011.

Zoehfeld, Kathleen Weidner. *Little Kids First Big Book of Science*. National Geographic, 2019.

AGES 7 TO 10

Drimmer, Stephanie Warren. *Ultimate Mammalpedia*. National Geographic, 2023.

Drimmer, Stephanie Warren. *Ultimate Weatherpedia*. National Geographic, 2019.

Lessem, Don. *Ultimate Dinopedia,* 2nd edition. National Geographic, 2017.

Murawski, Darlyne, and Nancy Honovich. *Ultimate Bugopedia*, 2nd edition. National Geographic, 2024.

Tomecek, Steve. *Ultimate Rockopedia*. National Geographic, 2020.

Wilsdon, Christina. *Ultimate Oceanpedia*. National Geographic, 2016.

Wilsdon, Christina. *Ultimate Predatorpedia*. National Geographic, 2018.

Wilsdon, Christina. *Ultimate Reptileopedia*. National Geographic, 2015.

Wilsdon, Christina, Patricia Daniels, and Jen Agresta. *Ultimate Bodypedia*. National Geographic, 2014.

ATLASES

National Geographic Kids My First Atlas of the World, 3rd edition. National Geographic, 2023.
(Ages 3–6)

National Geographic Kids Beginner's World Atlas, 5th edition. National Geographic, 2022.
(Ages 7–10)

National Geographic Kids World Atlas, 7th edition. National Geographic, 2025.
(Ages 11–14)

National Geographic Student World Atlas, 6th edition. National Geographic, 2022.
(Ages 15–18)

National Geographic Kids Beginner's United States Atlas, 4th edition. National Geographic, 2023.
(Ages 7–10)

National Geographic Kids United States Atlas, 7th edition. National Geographic, 2023.
(Ages 11–14)

PARENT TIPS

Extend your child's experience beyond the pages of this book. Every day can be filled with opportunities to learn more about almost everything!

JOINT EFFORT
(HUMAN BODY)

With your child, find and count the places in your bodies where two bones are joined so you can move. How many joints are in each hand? Each foot? Which joints do you use when you jump? When you shoot a basketball? When you mix a bowl of cookie dough?

WATCH IT GROW!
(BOTANY/PLANTS)

Have your child fill three cups or small pots with soil, add a few bean seeds to each, and water lightly. Place one in bright sun, one in shade, and one in a dark cabinet. Water each cup a bit every day. Check and record the growth. Talk with your child about the differences in growing conditions. How do the differences affect growth? Measure the size of the plants and record the measurements.

CLASSIFICATION STATION
(ANIMALS)

Take a trip to a zoo, aquarium, nature museum, or outdoor trail. Bring a notebook with a page marked for each of these different kinds of animals: mammals, birds, reptiles, amphibians, fish and mollusks, insects and arachnids. For each animal you see, have your child write its name or draw a picture on the appropriate page.

EXPLORE MYTHS
(CULTURAL ANTHROPOLOGY)

At your local library, your child can choose a book about myths and traditional stories. Such stories have been passed down for thousands of years, and they contain lessons that still hold true today. Once your child has selected a story, read it aloud together. Then have them act out their favorite scene. The two of you can put together a simple costume for even more fun!

TRASH INTO TREASURE
(ART, ENVIRONMENTAL AWARENESS)

Collect boxes, cans, bottles, and other clean trash with your child. What kind of sculpture can they create with these materials? Suggest different ways of holding things together, such as glue, rubber bands, or tape. Can your child build a sculpture taller than they are? How about something that is useful?

SUNRISE, SUNSET
(ASTRONOMY)

Go outside with your child in the morning to watch the sunrise. In the evening, watch the sunset together. To demonstrate why sunrise and sunset occur, stick a wooden skewer through the center of an apple. This represents Earth on its axis. Then put a pushpin in the apple to represent where you live. In a dark room, have your child set a flashlight on a table. Have them hold the skewer at an angle so that the light shines on the pin. Now have your child slowly turn the skewer. When the pin moves into the dark, that's sunset. When the pin comes back into the light, that's sunrise.

INDEX

Boldface indicates illustrations.

PHOTO CREDITS

Illustrations throughout by Sara Lynn Cramb/Astound US Inc unless otherwise noted below.

AD=Adobe Stock; AL=Alamy Stock Photo; DRMS=Dreamstime; GI=Getty Images; NGIC=National Geographic Image Collection; NGP=National Geographic Partners, LLC; SS=Shutterstock

Front Cover: (bird), Passakorn Umpornmaha/SS; (astronaut), Capitano Footage/SS; (Earth), max dallocco/AD; (dinosaur), Franco Tempesta/© NGP; (insect), tea maeklong/SS; (koala), Eric Isselée/SS; (King Tut's mask), kivandam/SS; (bulldozer), Anoo/AD; (rock crystal), afitz/AD; (Statue of Liberty), James Cheadle/AL; (flower), Ian 2010/SS; **Spine:** (koala), Eric Isselée/SS; **Back Cover:** (penguin), Eric Isselée/AD; (pumpkin), Leigh Prather/AD; (butterfly), Milous Chab/DRMS; (ant), Alekss/AD; **Front Matter:** 1, Eric Isselée/SS; 4 (weather icons), Anna Frajtova/AD; 4 (green rock), Björn Wylezich/AD; 4 (food illustrations), Sudowoodo/SS; 4 (umbrella), Elnur/DRMS; 4 (mother and daughter), Rido/AD; 4 (bacteria), Andy Frith/SS; 5 (compass), Andrey Kuzmin/AD; 5 (ant and ladybug), alekseyvanin/AD; 5 (penguin), Klein and Hubert/Minden Pictures; 5 (globe), Megarupa/SS; 5 (mushroom), Arie v.d. Wolde/SS; 5 (bee), rob2588/AD; 5 (shark), frantisek hojdysz/AD; 5 (duckling), Gregory Johnston/SS; 5 (giraffe), Heinrich van den Berg/Gallo Images/GI; 6 (dinosaur footprints), OlgaChernyak/SS; 6 (King Tut's mask), Kenneth Garrett/NGIC; 6 *(Pteranodon)*, Mark Turner/AL; 6 (Zeus), Chip Wass; 6 *(Patagotitan)*, Mohamad Haghani/AL; 6 (fern), guliveris/AD; 6 (palm leaves), Laboko/DRMS; 6 (paint palette), Vector Tradition/AD; 6 (smartphone), Mykyta/AD; 6 (scientist), yusufdemirci/AD; 6 (music notes), Graficriver/AD; 7 (airplane), MrVitkin/SS; 7 (satellite), phonlamaiphoto/AD; 7 (hot-air balloon), venusvi/AD; 7 (car), Andrey_Lobachev/AD; 7 (sailboat), Pixteegraph/AD; 7 (astronaut), Vladi333/SS; 7 (skate-boarder), Tomasz Trojanowski/AD; **Chapter 1:** 8-9 (girl with kite), graphic-line/SS; 8-9 (watercolor paper background throughout), Kues/SS; 8 (x-ray), Colorfuel Studio/AD; 8 (girl jumping), Henrik Sorensen/GI; 8 (boy on bike), Ljupco Smokovski/SS; 8 (banana), Graficriver/AD; 8 (basketball), freshidea/AD; 10 (LO LE), StockImageFactory/SS; 10 (RT), michaeljung/SS; 11 (CTR), Q88/SS; 12 (LO RT), GOLFX/SS; 16 (RT), WDnet Studio/AD; 17 (RT), Tom Wang/SS; 19 (bacteria), Andy Frith/SS; 19 (UP RT), Padop/SS; 20 (LO LE), grey_and/SS; 21 (LE), Anurak Pongpatimet/SS; 21 (LO LE), Andrew Angelov/SS; 21 (LO RT), kornnphoto/SS; 22, Gregg Vignal/AL; 22 (LO RT), neal and molly jansen/AL; 23 (UP), Ekaterina Pokrovsky/SS; 23 (UP RT), Tony Campbell/AD; 23 (LE), marigo20/SS; 23 (CTR), Designua/SS; 23 (loop, whorl, and arch), Maria Kalashnik/Alamy Stock Vector; 23 (thumb), Sylvia sooyoN/SS; 23 (fingerprint), andriano.cz/SS; 24 (music notes), Aleksandr_Lysenko/SS; 24 (CTR), Tom Wang/AL; 24 (LO), Wavebreakmedia/AD; 24 (UP RT), Alecsandr77/SS; 25 (UP LE), Dmitry Lobanov/SS; 25 (UP RT), VStock/AL; 25 (LE), Eric Isselée/SS; 25 (RT), Nataliia Zhekova/SS; 25 (LO RT), jehsomwang/SS; 26 (UP), Philip Pound/AL; 26 (LO), Caia Image/GI; 27 (UP LE), Christian Stoll/AD; 27 (CTR), BNP Design Studio/AL; 27 (RT), José Manuel Gelpi Díaz/AL; 27 (LO LE), Daniel Cole/Alamy Stock Vector; 27 (1, 2, 4), antto/AD; 27 (3), SpicyTruffel/AD; 28-29 (food illustrations), Sudowoodo/SS; 28-29 (food photos), Elena Schweitzer/SS; 29 (avocado), Floortje/SS; 30 (UP), Ljupco Smokovski/SS; 30 (LE), Aflo Co. Ltd./AL; 30 (RT), Sergey Novikov/AD; 30 (LO LE), Colorfuel Studio/SS; 30 (LO RT), Africa Studio/AD; 31 (UP), GoodStudio/SS; 31 (LE), photo_mts/AD; 31 (RT), chika_milan/AD; 31 (LO LE), Neil Tyers/SS; 31 (LO RT), Rido/AD; 32-33, MoMo Productions/GI; 32 (LO LE), Oleksandr Pokusai/AD; 33 (UP), Asian People Stock Photo/SS; 33 (UP RT), JGI/Jamie Grill/GI; 33 (CTR), Gabriela Insuratelu/AL; 33 (RT), nathapolHPS/SS; 33 (LO), Littlekidmoment/SS; 34 (happy Earth), dulya/AD; 34 (UP RT), Science Photo Library/Science Source; 34 (LO), Science Photo Library/AL; 35 (UP LE), Callista Images/Connect Images/AL; 35 (UP RT), Science Photo Library-Steve Gschmeissner/GI; 35 (CTR), James Ebanks/SS; 35 (LO LE), Peter Schupbach/Science Source; 35 (LO RT), DIgilife/AD; **Chapter 2:** 36 (coral), Dmitry/AD; 36 (windy cloud), John T Takai/SS; 36 (water drop), Pixel-Shot/AD; 36 (pink granite), Fabrizio Troiani/AL; 36-37 (mountain sketch), aluna1/AD; 37 (clouds), Culombio/AD; 37 (earth), 1xpert/AD; 37 (flower), An Nguyen/SS; 37 (chipmunk), dimj/AD; 38 (CTR), Beginning_artist/SS; 38 (LO), BlueRingMedia/SS; 40 (UP RT), Neoncat/AD; 40 (CTR), NG Maps; 40 (LO LE, CTR, and RT), BarksJapan/Alamy Stock Vector; 41 (UP LE), alejandro/AD; 41 (UP RT), Zephyr/Science Source; 41 (LO LE), Fer/AD; 41 (LO RT), momo2oki/AD; 42-43 (LE), bluering-media/AD; 43 (UP LE), Ralf Lehmann/SS; 43 (UP RT), JoseLuis/AD; 43 (CTR), vichie81/AD; 43 (LO RT), Zamir/AD; 43 (LO LE), Tom Nevesely/AD; 44 (UP RT), William Cunningham/AL; 44 (UP LE), Fabrizio Troiani/AL; 44 (CTR LE), Derek Croucher/AL; 44 (CTR RT), jon manjeot/AD; 44 (LO LE), Siim Sepp/AL; 44 (LO RT), Jay Beiler/DRMS; 46 (sunglasses), teploleta/AD; 46 (UP RT), siimsepp/AD; 46 (LE), vencav/AD; 46 (LO), Givaga/AD; 47 (UP LE), cevahir87/AD; 47 (UP RT), vvoe/AD; 47 (CTR LE), vvoe/AD; 47 (CTR RT), michal812/AD; 47 (LO LE), Alex Bogatyrev/SS; 47 (LO RT), boonchai sakunchonruedee/SS; 48 (UP LE), luchschenF/SS; 48 (UP RT), optimarc/SS; 48 (CTR RT), Madeleine Steinbach/AD; 48 (LO LE), J. Palys/SS; 48 (LO RT), Albert Russ/SS; 49 (UP LE), Mehmet Gokhan Bayhan/AD; 49 (UP RT), Björn Wylezich/AD; 49 (UP CTR LE), J.C.Salvadores/AD; 49 (LO CTR LE), Björn Wylezich/AD; 49 (CTR RT), Sebastian/AD; 49 (LO LE), Potapov Alexander/SS; 49 (LO RT), Imfoto/SS; 50 (UP), Celli07/AD; 50 (UP CTR), Song_about_summer/AD; 50 (LO CTR), Haico/AD; 50 (LO), Tom Fenske/AD; 51 (UP), Thierry RYO/AD; 51 (UP CTR), Jag_cz/AD; 51 (LO CTR), Kristian/AD; 51 (LO), Grafvision/AD; 52-53 (UP), belyay/AD; 52 (CTR LE), FattalPhotography/AD; 52 (CTR RT), YG Studio/AD; 52 (LE), blueringmedia/AD; 52 (LO RT), JayL/SS; 52 (squirrel), Alfmaler/AD; 53 (UP RT), jon manjeot/AD; 53 (CTR LE), Mongkolchon/AD; 53 (cactus), beskovaekaterina/AD; 53 (LO LE), anankkml/AD; 53 (LO RT), Wayne/SS; 55 (liquid), Cozine/SS; 55 (solid), kichigin19/AD; 55 (gas), Toa55/SS; 56 (UP RT), CE Photography/SS; 56 (LO LE), kredo/SS; 56 (LO RT), Patryk Kosmider/AD; 57 (UP), karnizz/AD; 57 (CTR LE), Christophe Testi/SS; 57 (CTR RT), Sergey Fedoskin/AD; 57 (LO), James McLaughlin/AL; 58 (UP LE), Peathegee Inc/GI; 58 (UP RT), Ivan Kmit/AD; 58 (CTR RT), Roman Khomlyak/SS; 58 (LO LE), Romolo Tavani/AD; 58 (LO RT), malcev852/AD; 58 (snowflake), Kebon doodle/AD; 58-59 (weather icons), Anna Frajtova/AD; 59 (UP), Elnur/DRMS; 59 (UP LE), Oliver Henze/AL; 59 (UP RT), Steven Love/AL; 59 (CTR), Irina Dmitrienko/AL; 59 (LO LE), Igumnova Irina/SS; 59 (LO RT), Alex Cimbal/SS; 60, yusufdemirci/AD; 61 (UP LE), Li Ding/AD; 61 (UP RT), Beata Predko/AL; 61 (CTR LE), Dudarev Mikhail/SS; 61 (CTR RT), Ivan Kmit/AD; 61 (LO LE), Valerii Shkliaev/SS; 61 (flower), An Nguyen/SS; 61 (snowflake), kichigin19/AD; 62 (UP), vadim_ozz/AD; 62 (LO), Alvina Labsvirs/AL; 63 (UP LE), Naeemphotographer2/SS; 63 (UP RT), muratart/SS; 63 (CTR), matteo_it/SS; 63 (LO LE), suronin/SS; 63 (LO RT), Andrii Vergeles/AD; **Chapter 3:** 64 (orangutan), Eric Isselée/SS; 64 (compass), Andrey Kuzmin/AD; 64 (globe sketch), Megarupa/SS; 65 (map sketch), ohmega1982/AD; 65 (girl in play boat), StoryTime Studio/SS; 65 (tower of Pisa), Roman Gorielov/AD; 66-67, NG Maps; 67 (LO RT), PondLord/AD; 68-69, NG Maps; 69 (UP RT), WavebreakmediaMicro/AD; 70-71, NG Maps; 70 (hot spring), Kris Wiktor/SS; 70 (bison), Olivier Le Queinec/SS; 70 (wolf), John Knight/GI; 70 (single butterfly), Sari ONeal/SS; 70 (butterflies), JHVEPhoto/AD; 71 (UP CTR), All Canada Photos/AD; 71 (UP RT), Colin/AD; 71 (alligator), dangdumrong/SS; 71 (CTR RT), Greg Amptman/SS; 72-73, NG Maps; 72 (UP LE), Bill Gozansky/AL; 72 (CTR), Steve Bloom Images/AL; 72 (LO LE), vitmark/AD; 73 (UP), Super Prin/SS; 73 (monkeys), Miguel Schmitter/SS; 73 (UP RT), Curioso.Photography/AD; 73 (capybaras), Steve Meese/SS; 73 (LO LE), Aziz Ary Neto/Connect Images/AL; 74-75, NG Maps; 74 (UP), Jordi De Rueda Roigé/AL; 74 (UP LE), Phase4Photography/AD; 74 (CTR LE), funkyfood London - Paul Williams/AL; 74 (LO LE), Givaga/AL; 74 (LO RT), g215/SS; 75 (UP), Renato Granieri/AL; 75 (UP RT), TTstudio/AD; 75 (CTR RT), alexmu/AD; 75 (LO LE), Sorin Colac/AL; 76-77, NG Maps; 76 (UP LE), Ivan Soto Cobos/SS; 76 (CTR LE), Liba Taylor/AL; 76 (LO LE), Stu Porter/AL; 76 (LO RT), Matthew/AD; 77 (UP), WitR/SS; 77 (Nile), Frontpage/SS; 77 (CTR RT), Dudarev Mikhail/SS; 77 (CTR), taboga/SS; 78-79, NG Maps; 78 (UP), Hakan Tanak/AD; 78 (CTR LE), Ryan Rodrick Beiler/AL; 78 (LO LE), Belikova Oksana/SS; 78 (LO), Travel Stock/SS; 79 (UP), Andrei Gilbert/AL; 79 (UP RT), kuzenkova/AD; 79 (CTR), Hung Chung Chih/SS; 79 (CTR RT), James Kelley/AD; 79 (LO LE), Anan Kaewkhammul/AL; 80-81, NG Maps; 80 (UP LE), leelakajonkij/AD; 80 (CTR LE), Uwe Aranas/SS; 80 (LO), Pete Niesen/SS; 81 (koalas), worldswildlifewonders/SS; 81 (kangaroo), Thorsten Milse/Robert Harding/AL; 81 (CTR), Doug Houghton/AL; 81 (LO CTR), Guillem/AD; 81 (LO), Joel Sartore/Photo Ark/NGIC; 82-83, NG Maps; 82 (UP), Mike/AD; 82 (CTR LE), Ashley Cooper/AL; 82 (LO LE), Klein and Hubert/Minden Pictures; 82 (LO RT), Silver/AD; 83 (UP), hecke71/AD; 83 (UP CTR), Jeronimo Saravia/Wirestock/AD; 83 (CTR), paolo gislimberti/AL; 83 (LO LE), Jason Edwards/AL; 84-85, NG Maps; **Chapter 4:** 86-87 (textured background), leekhoailang/AD; 86-87 (farm sketch), mozart3737/AD; 86 (hummingbird), Rob Jansen/SS; 86 (mushroom), WinWin artlab/SS; 86 (oranges), Iryna Denysova/SS; 86 (strawberry), Maks Narodenko/SS; 86 (bee), rob2588/AD; 87 (goat), Shotprime Studio/AD; 87 (tree), Production Perig/AD; 88 (UP), Triff/SS; 88 (CTR), hadkhanong/AD; 88 (LO LE), Anna Giovenzana/SS; 88-89 (CTR), WinWin/AD; 89 (UP), Taigi/AL; 89 (CTR), Fernando/AD; 89 (LO), Oleg Malshakov/AD; 91 (LO RT), dule964/AD; 93 (UP LE), Bill Gozansky/AL; 93 (UP RT), mhgstan/AD; 93 (CTR), annette shaff/AD; 93 (CTR RT), William Leaman/AL; 93 (LO LE), John Richmond/AL; 93 (LO RT), Peter Atkinson/AL; 94 (UP LE), Chayata/SS; 94 (UP RT), J Maas/peopleimages/AD; 94 (LO LE), LorraineHudgins/SS; 94 (LO RT), Stephen Harrison/AL; 95 (dog), Jackan/SS; 95 (burrs), wasanajai/SS; 95 (walnuts), Valentyn Volkov/AL; 95 (peas), Tiger Images/SS; 95 (peanuts), Hong Vo/SS; 95 (cashews), Pongphan Ruengchai/AL; 95 (pomegranate), Maks Narodenko/SS; 95 (lentils), Madlen/SS; 95 (pistachios), Zoonar/Vladimir Blinov/AL; 95 (green pistachio), Tanya_mtv/SS; 95 (Himalayan balsam), blickwinkel/AL; 95 (corn), Serg64/SS; 96 (UP LE), thanongsak22/SS; 96 (UP RT), Anita Kainrath/SS; 96 (LO LE), Nick Taurus/AD; 96 (LO RT), LHBLLC/SS; 97 (UP LE), Faiz Fahminudin/SS; 97 (UP RT), Sirinn3249/SS; 97 (CTR RT), wu kailiang/AL; 97 (LO LE), CathyKeifer/GI; 97 (LO RT), Videowokart/SS; 98 (CTR), Vladitto/SS; 98 (LO LE), spacezerocom/AD; 99 (UP), Xalanx/AD; 99 (CTR), Cuu Pha Le Nguyen/AL; 99 (LO LE), srekap/AD; 99 (LO RT), srekap/AD; 102 (dragon fruit), Crepesoles/SS; 102 (CTR LE), LianeM/SS; 102 (RT), Anton Starikov/AL; 102 (pineapple slice), Jurij Kachkovskij/AL; 102 (strawberry), Maks Narodenko/SS; 102 (LO LE), andrewhagen/AD; 103 (UP LE), Hongyan/AD; 103 (UP CTR), rodimovpavel/AD; 103 (UP RT), Valentyn Volkov/AL; 103 (LO LE), Giuma/AD; 103 (LO CTR), ICP/incamerastock/AL; 103 (LO RT), grey/AD; 104 (UP), Gertjan Hooijer/SS; 104 (LO LE), Anne Powell/SS; 104 (LO RT), Fotografiecor/SS; 105 (UP LE), Jamikorn Sooktaramorn/SS; 105 (UP RT), Martin J. Calabrese/SS; 105 (CTR RT), CampSmoke/SS; 105 (LO), Arie v.d. Wolde/SS; 108 (happy Earth), dulya/AD; 108 (LE), Naokita/AD; 108 (RT), Stephen/AD; 109 (UP LE), Robert Bush/AL; 109 (UP RT), goodgold99/SS; 109 (CTR LE), cn0ra/AD; 109 (LO LE), Adam Jones/Danita Delimont/AL; 109 (LO RT), jovannig/AD; **Chapter 5:** 110 (snake), Dmitry/AD; 110 (giraffe), Heinrich van den Berg/Gallo Images/GI; 110 (monkey), JackF/AD; 111 (polar bear), Olga Prozorova/AD; 111 (iceberg sketch), aluna1/AD; 111 (penguin), Klein and Hubert/Minden Pictures; 111 (iceberg), Lucky_Graphic & AI/AD; 112 (shrew), Daniel Heuclin/Nature Picture Library; 112 (African landscape), Vector_Up/SS; 112 (LO), Frans Lanting/NGIC; 113 (animal prints), Design Studio RM/AD; 113 (UP), chamnan phanthong/AD; 113 (CTR LE), MyImages - Micha/SS; 113 (CTR RT), Podarenka/AD; 113 (LO), Andrea Izzotti/SS; 114 (UP LE), Alfmaler/AD; 114-115 (UP), Betty Sederquist/AD; 114 (CTR LE), annette shaff/AD; 114 (LO), Eric Isselée/AD; 114 (plants), Oceloti/AD; 114 (throughout), Design Studio RM/AD; 115 (polar bear), volkova natalia/SS; 115 (polar bear cub), Eric Isselée/AD; 115 (CTR LE), Mikael Males/AL; 115 (LO RT), fotomaster/AD; 115 (LO LE), Ondrej Prosicky/SS; 116 (LE), Eric Isselée/SS; 116-117 (branches), schondrienn/AD; 116 (UP RT), Kevin Schafer/AL; 116 (LO RT), Dominik Rueß/AD; 117 (UP RT), Craig Ingram/AL; 117 (UP LE), IrinaK/SS; 117 (animal prints), Design Studio RM/AD; 117 (LO), Anan Kaewkhammul/AL; 118 (UP LE), fotomaster/AD; 118 (UP RT), Doug Lindstrand/Alaska Stock RF/Design Pics Inc/AL; 118 (LO), Dario Pautasso/SS; 118 (background), ActiveLines/AD; 119 (animal prints), Design Studio RM/AD; 119 (UP), Arco/TUNS/imageBROKER/AL; 119 (RT), vencav/AD; 119 (CTR), Anan Kaewkhammul/AL; 119 (CTR LE), kwadrat70/AD; 119 (LO), byrdyak/AD; 120 (UP LE), Edwin Butter/AD; 120 (UP RT), Chien Lee/Minden Pictures; 120-121 (mandrill), Eric Isselée/AD; 120 (LO LE), Ronan Donovan/NGIC; 121 (UP LE), Janette Hill/Robert Harding; 121 (UP RT), Sergio Pitamiz/Robert Harding; 121 (CTR), Joel Sartore/Photo Ark/NGIC; 121 (LO RT), Lori Epstein/NGIC; 124 (UP), Alex Mustard/Nature Picture Library/AL; 124 (LO LE), Joerg Reuther/imageBROKER/Biosphoto; 124 (LO RT), Brian Parker/AL; 124 (plant), Iuliia/AD; 125 (UP), Todd Mintz/AL; 125 (CTR), Mats/AD; 125 (LO), Life on white/AL; 126 (UP LE), Allakuly-evva/AD; 126 (UP RT), Lilifox/AD; 126 (LE), Olhastock/SS; 126 (LO RT), Dudarev Mikhail/SS; 126-127 (background), imagination13/AD; 127 (UP LE), Gregory Johnston/SS; 127 (UP RT), Michael Verbeek/AD; 127 (CTR LE), Helga Madajova/SS; 127 (LO), Baronb/SS; 128 (UP), Michal Sikorski/AL; 128 (LO LE), Wildphotos/DRMS; 128 (LO RT), Ann and Steve Toon/Robert Harding/AL; 129 (UP LE), Fred Lord/AL; 129 (UP RT), Arto Hakola/AL;

129 (LO LE), Guy Bryant/AD; 129 (LO RT), Ondrej Prosicky/SS; 130 (UP), Wang LiQiang/SS; 130 (CTR LE), Ivan Kuzmin/AL; 130 (CTR), photomaster/SS; 130 (CTR RT), Andre Seah Photography/Wirestock Creators/AD; 130 (LO LE), mihirjoshi/SS; 131 (UP RT), Albert Beukhof/SS; 131 (CTR), Harry Collins Photography/SS; 131 (LE), Phant/SS; 131 (CTR RT), FJAH/SS; 131 (LO), Ondrej Prosicky/SS; 132 (UP LE), creativeteam/AD; 132 (CTR), David Tipling/David Tipling Photo Library/AL; 133 (UP), Ken Griffiths/AL; 133 (CTR), Lei Zhu NZ/AD; 133 (CTR RT), Eric Isselée/SS; 133 (LO LE), blickwinkel/Wothe/AL; 133 (LO RT), Life on white/AL; 136 (UP), Robert Wyatt/AL; 136 (CTR RT), Massimo Piacentino/AL; 136 (CTR LE), Rod Williams/Nature Picture Library; 136 (LO), A Periam Photography/SS; 137 (UP), Gone For A Drive/AD; 137 (CTR), PetlinDmitry/SS; 137 (LO), Astira/AD; 138 (UP LE), creativeteam/AD; 138 (CTR), Bence Mate/Nature Picture Library/AL; 138 (LO), gudkovandrey/AD; 139 (UP LE), André Gilden/AL; 139 (UP RT), imageBROKER/Marko von der Osten/AL; 139 (CTR RT), Joe Blossom/AL; 139 (LO RT), Agus_Gatam/SS; 139 (LO LE), KAMONRAT/SS; 140 (UP LE), Vectors Market/AD; 140 (CTR RT), Grispb/AD; 140 (CTR LE), Catchlight Lens/SS; 140-141 (LO), blickwinkel/McPHOTO/PUM/AL; 141 (UP LE), Michael Patrick O'Neill/AL; 141 (UP RT), Tony Campbell/AD; 144 (UP), imageBROKER GmbH & Co. KG/AL; 144 (LO LE), Eric Isselée/SS; 144 (LO RT), reptiles4all/SS; 144-147 (frog prints), EVGENIY/AD; 145 (UP), South12th Photography/SS; 145 (CTR), Narek87/SS; 145 (LO), Milan Zygmunt/AL; 146 (lily pads), Igarts/AD; 146 (CTR), trgrowth/SS; 147 (CTR), bartsadowski/AD; 147 (leaves), HakujiHaruka/AD; 148 (UP), Norbert Probst/imageBROKER GmbH & Co. KG/AL; 148 (LO LE), Alexander Raths/SS; 148 (LO RT), Michael Patrick O'Neill/AL; 149 (UP LE), imageBROKER/R.Dirscherl/AL; 149 (UP RT), Sahara Frost/AD; 149 (CTR RT), Helmut Corneli/AL; 149 (CTR), Terry Moore/Stocktrek Images/AL; 149 (LO), Marko Steffensen/AL; 150 (UP), Reinhard Dirscherl/AL; 150 (CTR), Picture Partners/SS; 150 (LO), michaelgeyer/AD; 150-151 (UP), frantisek hojdysz/AD; 151 (CTR), crisod/AD; 151 (CTR RT), Marko Steffensen/AL; 151 (LO LE), WaterFrame_mus/AL; 151 (LO RT), wildestanimal/AD; 154 (UP), Handies Peak/AD; 154 (CTR), Luke Suen/iStockphoto; 154 (LO LE), Blue Planet Archive WPO/AL; 154 (LO RT), Johan Swanepoel/AL; 155 (UP LE), Momo5287/SSk; 155 (UP RT), George Grall/AL; 155 (CTR LE), mashe/SS; 155 (CTR RT), Solvin Zankl/Minden Pictures; 155 (LO), SeaTops/AL; 156-157 (ants and spiders), alekseyvanin/AD; 156 (UP), chas53/AD; 156 (ant), Henrik Larsson/SS; 156 (bee), Daniel Prudek/AD; 156 (LO), Lutsenko_Oleksandr/SS; 157 (UP LE), Luis Quinta/Nature Picture Library; 157 (UP RT), Damian O. Elias/NGIC; 157 (LO LE), cliff collings/SS; 157 (LO RT), Eric Isselée/SS; 158-159 (ladybugs and flies), alekseyvanin/AD; 158 (UP), Stefan Holm/SS; 158 (CTR), Skip Moody/Dembinsky Photo Associates/AL; 158 (LO), constantincornel/AD; 159 (UP LE), Ivan Kuzmin/AD; 159 (UP RT), Milous Chab/DRMS; 159 (LO LE), Valeriy Kirsanov/AD; 159 (fly), Alekss/AD; 159 (LO RT), Dr. Torsten Heydenreich/imageBROKER GmbH & Co. KG/AL; 160-161 (CTR), JuliaBliznyakova/AD; 160 (ants), Antrey/AD; 160 (CTR LE), JJ van Ginkel/AL; 161 (UP), kozorog/AD; 161 (LO), Paul Williams/Nature Picture Library; 162 (happy Earth), dulya/AD; 162 (UP RT), Gaertner/ALo; 162 (CTR), outdoorsman/SS; 162 (LO LE), Zeeshan Mirza/ephotocorp/AL; 162 (LO RT), Arco/F. Schneider/ImageBROKER/AL; 163 (UP LE), louise murray/AL; 163 (UP RT), Peter Tsai Photography/AL; 163 (CTR LE), Cheattha/AD; 163 (LO LE), Christina L. Evans/Rainbow/RGB Ventures/SuperStock/AL; 163 (LO RT), ODell Outside/AD; **Chapter 6:** 164-165 (rainforest), Natalia/AD; 164 (leaves), Baurz1973/SS; 164 (small dino), Seamartini/Alamy Stock Vector; 164 (dino prints), OlgaChernyak/SS; 164 *(Brachiosaurus)*, warpaintcobra/AD; 164 (fossil), Mark Brandon/SS; 165 *(Quetzalcoatlus)*, Friedrich Saurer/AL; 165 *(Spinosaurus)*, photosvac/AD; 165 (volcano sketch), Danussa/AD; 166 (UP LE), Marie Sprunger/AL; 166 *(Archaeopteryx)*, Catmando/SS; 166 (LE), Franco Tempesta/NGP; 166 (fern), guliveris/AD; 166-167 (*Hualianceratops* and *Guanlong*), Franco Tempesta/NGP; 167 (dino icon), Kristina Chistiakova/AD; 167 (alligator), Eric Isselée/AD; 167 (viper), Monaris/SS; 167 (turtle), cynoclub/AD; 167 (leaves), oradige59/SS; 167 (CTR), Mohamad Haghani/AL; 168 (UP), Franco Tempesta/NGP; 168 (LO), Franco Tempesta/© NGP; 169 (UP), Encyclopaedia Britannica/Universal Images Group North America LLC/AL; 169 (CTR LE), Warpaint/SS; 169 (CTR RT), Franco Tempesta/© NGP; 169 (LO LE), Franco Tempesta/© NGP; 169 (LO RT), Franco Tempesta/© NGP; 170 (leaves), Laboko/DRMS; 170 (ginkgo), Nenov Brothers/AD; 170 (CTR LE), warpaintcobra/AD; 170 (CTR RT), Mark Turner/AL; 170 (LO), warpaintcobra/AD; 170 (trumpet), Tarasenko Maksym/DRMS; 170 (LO RT), guliveris/AD; 171 (UP), leonello calvetti/AL; 171 (CTR LE), warpaintcobra/AD; 171 (CTR RT), Franco Tempesta/© NGP; 171 (LO), Nobumichi Tamura/Stocktrek Images/AL; 172 (UP), Mark Turner/AL; 172 (LO LE), Chris Masnaghetti/Paleostock; 172 (LO RT), The Hoberman Collection/AL; 173 (UP LE), Michael Rosskothen/AD; 173 (UP RT), Friedrich Saurer/AL; 173 (CTR), Mark Turner/AL; 173 (LO LE), Mark Garlick/Science Photo Library/AL; 173 (LO RT), Roger Harris/Science Photo Library/AL; 174 (CTR), Sumit buranarothtrakul/SS; 174 (tools), Dorling Kindersley ltd/AL; 174 (LO), Akkharat J./AD; 175 (UP LE), Dotted Yeti/SS; 175 (UP RT), Tom & Therisa Stack; 175 (CTR LE), GL Archive/AL; 175 (CTR RT), David Buzzard/SS; 175 (LO), lassedesignen/AD; 178 (happy Earth), dulya/AD; 178 (UP), Franco Tempesta/© NGP; 178 (LO), Elenarts/SS; 179 (UP), Daniel Eskridge/AD; 179 (CTR), Franco Tempesta/© NGP; 179 (LO LE), Herschel Hoffmeyer/SS; 179 (LO RT), Carlton Publishing Group/Science Source; **Chapter 7:** 180 (statues), dcylai/AD; 180 (Zeus), Chip Wass; 180 (Aztec calendar), PB/AD; 180 (totem), Dan Breckwoldt/SS; 180-181 (pyramid drawing), Joshy/AD; 181 (King Tut), Jaroslav Moravcik/AD; 181 (ankh), Yezepchyk Oleksandr/SS; 181 (sand texture), Yaran/AD; 182 (UP), Grant Faint/GI; 182 (LO), Ozja/SS; 182-183 (animal icons), nikiteev/AD; 183 (column), 4zevar/AD; 183 (UP), Paul/AD; 183 (CTR), Andrea Izzotti/AD; 183 (LO LE), Paul Moore/AD; 183 (LO RT), Pascal Goetgheluck/Science Source; 184-185, NG Maps; 184-185 (icons), Sara Lynn Cramb/Astound US Inc; 186-187 (CTR), Jon Bower Egypt/AL; 186 (LE), Kenneth Garrett/NGIC; 186-187 (ancient Egyptian symbols), topvectors/AD; 187 (UP), Pius Lee/DRMS; 187 (CTR RT), Konstantin Yolshin/SS; 187 (CTR), Rebecca Hale/NGIC; 187 (LO CTR), QBR/SS; 188 (UP LE), naty_lee/AD; 188 (CTR LE), David Davis Photoproductions RF/AL; 188 (CTR RT), cyc1980s/SS; 188 (LO LE), The History Collection/AL; 188 (LO RT), Dorling Kindersley/Dorling Kindersley ltd/AL; 189 (UP), Yuri Yavnik/SS; 189 (CTR LE), Studio-Annika/iStockphoto; 189 (CTR RT), JingAiping/SS; 189 (LO RT), incomible/AD; 190 (UP LE), Flash Vector/AD; 190 (CTR LE), Chip Wass; 190 (CTR RT), tilialucida/AD; 190 (LO LE), Repina Valeriya/AD; 190 (LO RT), Gift of El Conde de Lagunillas, 1956/The Metropolitan Museum of Art; 191 (UP LE), Karolina Maliszewska/AL; 191 (CTR RT), RuslanKphoto/SS; 191 (CTR), steeve-x-art/AL; 191 (LO LE), LianeM/SS; 191 (LO RT), Javier Espila/Shannon Associates; 192 (UP), Flash Vector/AD; 192 (CTR), Jesse Kraft/AL; 192 (LO LE), Eric Isselée/SS; 192 (LO RT), Lori Epstein/AL; 193 (UP), Harald von Radebrecht/imageBROKER GmbH & Co. KG/AL; 193 (CTR LE), Katya Palladina/Stockimo/AL; 193 (RT), Gift and Bequest of Alice K. Bache, 1974, 1977/The Metropolitan Museum of Art; 193 (CTR), The Michael C. Rockefeller Memorial Collection, Bequest of Nelson A. Rockefeller, 1979/The Metropolitan Museum of Art; 193 (LO LE), Gift and Bequest of Alice K. Bache, 1974, 1977/The Metropolitan Museum of Art; 194 (UP), Ian Dagnall/AL; 194 (LO LE), Rosanne Tackaberry/AL; 194 (LO RT), DEA/G. Cigolini/GI; 195 (UP), Aaron Huey/NGIC; 195 (RT), Dan Breckwoldt/SS; 195 (CTR), winterbilder/AD; 195 (CTR LE), The Charles and Valerie Diker Collection of Native American Art, Gift of Charles and Valerie Diker, 2019; 195 (LO), Kevin G Smith/Design Pics Inc/AL; 196 (UP LE), sabelskaya/AD; 196 (CTR), kovgabor79/AD; 196 (LO LE), wannasak saetia/SS; 196 (LO RT), demerzel21/AD; 197 (UP), Steve Raymer/NGIC; 197 (palm tree icon), Anna Frajtova/AD; 197 (CTR), oliver de la haye/AD; 197 (LO LE), AlexUm5/SS; 197 (LO RT), powerofforever/GI; 198 (happy Earth), dulya/AD; 198 (UP RT), Last Refuge/Robert Harding/AL; 198 (LO), Jan Wlodarczyk/AL; 199 (UP LE), Bule Sky Studio/SS; 199 (UP RT), Sorin Colac/AL; 199 (CTR), AP Photo/Martin Mejia; 199 (LO LE), Zev Radovan/BibleLandPictures/AL; 199 (LO RT), Kenneth Garrett/NGIC; **Chapter 8:** 200 (girl), Africa Studio/AD; 200 (glasses), cherezoff/AD; 200 (telescope), Taufiq/AD; 200 (popcorn), katyamaximenko/AD; 200 (popcorn kernels), Ilya Akinshin/SS; 200 (palette), BillionPhotos/AD; 200 (100-dollar bill), chones/AD; 200-201 (wind and solar energy sketch), yuromanovich/AD; 201 (tablet drawing), Jose/AD; 202-203 (throughout), VectorMine/AD; 202 (CTR), Pavel L Photo and Video/SS; 202 (CTR LE), Independent Picture Service/AL; 202 (LO), Daxiao Productions/AD; 203 (lightbulb icon throughout), Comauthor/AD; 203 (UP), Nomad_Soul/SS; 203 (CTR LE), webphotographeer/GI; 203 (CTR RT), thawatpong/AD; 203 (tractor), LesPalenik/SS; 203 (LO RT), Lachina/NGP; 204 (UP CTR), yusufdemirci/AD; 204 (UP RT), Pixel-Shot/AD; 204 (LE), Dmitriy Kostylev/SS; 204 (RT), Caia Image/GI; 204 (LO), Sodel Vladyslav/SS; 205 (UP LE), Kostikova Natalia/SS; 205 (UP RT), Alexander Potapov/AD; 205 (CTR LE), Science RF/AD; 205 (CTR RT), Rawpixel/AD; 205 (LO LE), Andrea Izzotti/AD; 205 (computer), vladwel/AD; 205 (LO RT), Num/AD; 206 (UP RT), ArtMari/SS; 207 (wind turbines), Simon Belcher/AL; 207 (dam), Rodphothong Mr. Patchara/SS; 207 (solar panels), Soonthorn/AD; 207 (coal mine), TTstudio/SS; 207 (coal), anat chant/SS; 208 (LE), graja/SS; 208 (UP RT), Hero Images/Adobe; 208 (LO RT), Preto Perola/SS; 209 (UP LE), New Africa/AD; 209 (UP CTR), cristi180884/SS; 209 (UP RT), Pressmaster/SS; 209 (CTR), Richard Peterson/SS; 209 (CTR LE), Ilya Akinshin/SS; 209 (shell), Denis Tabler/SS; 209 (cocoa beans), AmyLv/SS; 209 (100-dollar bill), chones/AD; 209 (LO), V.S. Anandhakrishna/SS; 210 (UP LE), Mykyta/AD; 210 (CTR LE), Quagga Media/AL; 210 (CTR RT), Everett Collection/SS; 210 (LO LE), Rawpixel/SS; 210 (LO RT), nopparada samrhubsuk/SS; 211 (UP LE), Niels Poulsen mus/AL; 211 (UP RT), zentilia/AD; 211 (CTR LE), Vasyl Shulga/SS; 211 (CTR RT), Photo Researchers/Science History Images/AL; 211 (LO CTR LE), Lori Epstein/National Geographic Partners; 211 (LO CTR), Lockie Currie/GI; 211 (LO LE), Cincila/SS; 211 (LO RT), vadymstock/AD; 212 (UP), khd/SS; 212 (UP CTR), Dariia/AD; 212 (LO LE), yxm2008/SS; 212 (LO RT), J.Enrique Molina/AL; 213 (UP), Library of Congress; 213 (CTR), Imaginechina-Tuchong/AL; 213 (LO LE), jantsarik/SS; 213 (LO RT), Dja65/SS; 214 (palette), Vector Tradition/AD; 214 (CTR), strekalova/AD; 214 (LO LE), Angelina Zinovieva/AD; 214 (LO RT), vvoe/SS; 215 (UP), emotionpicture/AD; 215 (CTR RT), Wendy Kaveney/AD; 215 (CTR), igor kisselev/SS; 215 (CTR LE), anek.soowannaphoom/SS; 215 (LO LE), Anna Averianova/SS; 215 (LO RT), all_about_people/SS; 216 (music notes), Graficriver/AD; 216 (UP RT), The Object Series/Visual Symbols; 216 (CTR LE), wavebreakmedia/SS; 216 (LO LE), Highwaystarz-Photography/GI; 216 (LO RT), Sunny_Smile/AD; 217 (UP LE), B Christopher/AL; 217 (UP RT), PeopleImages/GI; 217 (CTR LE), Aflo Images/GI; 217 (LO LE), Richard Levine/AL; 217 (LO RT), Agami Photo Agency/SS; 218 (UP LE), Vereshchagin Dmitry/SS; 218 (UP CTR), Tiler84/AD; 218 (UP RT), IndiaPix/AD; 218 (LO LE), BillionPhotos/AD; 218 (LO RT), Dmitry Vereshchagin/AD; 219 (UP LE), Kittichai/AD; 219 (UP RT), Wavebreakmedia Ltd/DRMS; 219 (CTR LE), sparkia/AD; 219 (CTR RT), Tarasenko Maksym/DRMS; 219 (LO LE), Boiko Y/SS; 219 (didgeridoo), Igal/AD; 219 (LO CTR), sonsedskaya/AD; 219 (LO RT), mhatzapa/SS; 220 (happy Earth), dulya/AD; 220 (UP), Andrij Vatsyk/SS; 220 (LO), EWY Media/SS; 221 (UP LE), Viagens e Caminhos/SS; 221 (UP RT), Tim Rooke/SS; 221 (CTR LE), Herr Loeffler/AD; 221 (CTR RT), saiko3p/AD; 221 (LO), imago images/Xinhua/AL; **Chapter 9:** 222 (train), aapsky/AD; 222 (speed lines), aonaka/AD; 222 (skateboarder), Tomasz Trojanowski/AD; 222 (dog in car), Jenny Sturm/AD; 223 (plane), Magicleaf/SS; 223 (hot-air balloon), venusvi/AD; 223 (sailboat), Pixteegraph/AD; 223 (wind icon), Arcady/AD; 223 (waves), Ihor/AD; 223 (car), Andrey_Lobachev/AD; 224 (UP RT), IfH/SS; 224 (CTR), coroiu octavian/AL; 224 (LO), GrashAlex/SS; 225 (UP LE), David Arment/AD; 225 (UP RT), New Africa/AD; 225 (CTR LE), PRILL Mediendesign/AD; 225 (CTR RT), Nerthuz/SS; 225 (LO), Jim Monk/AL; 226 (UP LE), Yuri Kevhiev/AL; 226 (UP RT), Olivier Renck/Aurora Open RF/Cavan Images/AL; 226 (LO LE), MichaelSvoboda/GI; 226 (LO RT), shital/AD; 227 (UP LE), Ljupco Smokovski/AD; 227 (UP RT), Monkey Business/AD; 227 (CTR LE), Taras Hipp/SS; 227 (CTR RT), Anton27/SS; 227 (LO LE), Denis Moskvinov/SS; 227 (LO RT), Ljupco Smokovski/AD; 228-229 (LE), David/AD; 228 (UP RT), Gopal3366/SS; 228 (LO LE), Sailorr/SS; 229 (UP), Locomotive74/SS; 229 (CTR RT), Taina Sohlman/SS; 229 (LO CTR RT), 26ShadesofGreen/AL; 229 (LO), S.Borisov/SS; 232 (UP RT), SNEHIT PHOTO/AD; 232 (CTR), Shannon Hibberd/NGIC; 233 (UP RT), noraismail/SS; 233 (UP LE), dotshock/SS; 233 (CTR), US Navy Photo/AL; 233 (LO LE), Glenn Aguilar/AL; 233 (LO RT), phaisarnwong2517/AD; 233 (waves), Vector/SS; 234 (UP), Sfio Cracho/AD; 234 (LO LE), GL Archive/AL; 234 (LO RT), topseller/SS; 235 (UP), Rene Hartmann/AD; 235 (RT), SpaceEnhanced/AL; 235 (CTR), MrVitkin/SS; 235 (LO LE), Anatoliy Lukich/SS; 236 (happy Earth), dulya/AD; 236-237, Yinan Zhang/DRMS; 236 (LO), Dan Wozniak/Southcreek Global/Zuma Press, Inc./AL; 237 (UP RT), Sipa USA/AL; 237 (CTR LE), Pedro Portal/El Nuevo Herald/Tribune News Service/Zuma Press; 237 (LO LE), David Parker/AL; 237 (LO RT), dpa picture alliance/AL; **Chapter 10:** 238 (rocket), Denis Rozhnovsky/AD; 239 (satellite), Oleksii Akhrimenko/AD; 239 (Saturn), Natural PNG/AD; 239 (astronaut), welsonhendra/AD; 239 (background), aluna1/AD; 240 (star field), Oleksandra/AD; 240 (satellite), phonlamaiphoto/AD; 241 (meteor), Muhammad Abu Dzar Al Ghifari/Alamy Stock Vector; 241 (plane), phive2015/AD; 241 (Earth), Jeremy Culp Design/AD; 243 (planet icon), luck/AD; 244 (happy sun), Sathaporn/AD; 244 (large sun), blickwinkel/McPHOTO/GAN/AL; 244 (sunspots), Claudio Caridi/AD; 244 (solar flare), solarseven/SS; 245 (UP RT), Sathaporn/AD; 245 (CTR), godrick/AL; 245 (LO), Delphotostock/AD; 246 (UP), oleon17/AD; 246 (CTR), Peter Jurik/AL; 246 (LO), Yuri Arcurs/AL; 247 (UP LE), Tandem Stock/AD; 247 (UP RT), Dennis Hallinan/AL; 247 (CTR RT), NASA Image Collection/AL; 247 (LO RT), Stocktrek Images, Inc./AL; 247 (CTR LE), Project with vigour/AFLO/AL; 247 (LO LE), PaulPaladin/AL; 248 (UP LE), Muhammad Abu Dzar Al Ghifari/Alamy Stock Vector; 248 (RT), James Thew/AL; 248 (LE), David Aguilar/National Geographic Partners; 248-249 (LO), AvDe/SS; 249 (UP), Ron Miller/Stocktrek Images/Science Source; 249 (CTR), Vladimir/AD; 250 (LE), Vladi333/SS; 250 (RT), Denis Rozhnovsky/AD; 250 (LO LE), Andrei Armiagov/SS; 250-251 (UP), Naeblys/SS; 251 (CTR), evgeniy/AD; 251 (RT), siraphat/SS; 251 (LO LE), dotted zebra/AL; 254 (happy Earth), dulya/AD; 254 (UP RT), Science RF/AD; 254 (LO), Irina Dmitrienko/AL; 255 (UP LE), Andrew Bret Wallis/GI; 255 (UP RT), It4All/AD; 255 (CTR), David Aguilar/National Geographic Partners; 255 (LO LE), Science History Images/AL; 255 (LO RT), Science History Images/AL; **Back Matter:** 258 (UP), Rob Jansen/SS; 258 (LO), Romolo Tavani/AD; 260 (UP), Manny DaCunha/AD; 260 (LO), hiphoto39/AD; 261 (UP), leungchopan/SS; 261 (CTR), Chinnapong/AD; 261 (LO), RTimages/AD

Since 1888, the National Geographic Society has funded more than 14,000 research, conservation, education, and storytelling projects around the world. National Geographic Partners distributes a portion of the funds it receives from your purchase to National Geographic Society to support programs including the conservation of animals and their habitats. To learn more, visit natgeo.com/info.

For more information, visit nationalgeographic.com, call 1-877-873-6846, or write to the following address:

National Geographic Partners, LLC
1145 17th Street NW
Washington, DC 20036-4688 U.S.A.

More for kids from National Geographic: natgeokids.com

National Geographic Kids magazine inspires children to explore their world with fun yet educational articles on animals, science, nature, and more. Using fresh storytelling and amazing photography, *Nat Geo Kids* shows kids ages 6 to 14 the fascinating truth about the world—and why they should care. natgeo.com/subscribe

For rights or permissions inquiries, please contact National Geographic Books Subsidiary Rights: bookrights@natgeo.com

Designed by Amanda Larsen, Julide Dengel, Lauren Sciortino, and David Marvin

Hardcover ISBN: 978-1-4263-7402-9
Reinforced library binding ISBN: 978-1-4263-7547-7

The publisher gratefully acknowledges Dr. Tovah P. Klein, director of the Barnard College Center for Toddler Development, for her advice and expertise. We are also grateful to the following academics, scientists, and subject matter experts for their review of this book: Anisha Abraham, M.D., Chief of Adolescent and Young Adult Medicine, Children's National; Rauri Bowie, Ph.D., Curator of Birds, Museum of Vertebrate Zoology, University of California Berkeley; Naomi R. Caldwell, Ramapough Lenape Nation and Ph.D., Montana State University, Bozeman; Liang Cai, Ph.D., University of Notre Dame; Rick Castle, Classics Ph.D., University of California Santa Barbara; Debra Colodner, Ph.D., Director of Conservation Education and Science, Arizona-Sonora Desert Museum; Anita Cook, Ph.D., Professor Emerita, Catholic University; Elissa Day, Ph.D. Student, Harvard University; Alden Ross Denny, Chief Geoscientist, ADEPTH Minerals; Laura Figueroa, Ph.D., University of Massachusetts Amherst; David Gruber, Ph.D., National Geographic Explorer; Linda Hardison, Ph.D., Director of OregonFlora, Oregon State University; Melissa Hawkins, Ph.D., Curator-in-Charge, Smithsonian Museum of Natural History; Ricardo Holdo, Ph.D., University of Georgia; Adele Igel, Ph.D., University of California Davis; Kale Kanaeholo, Ph.D. Student, University of Hawai'i at Mānoa; Adam Leaché, Ph.D., University of Washington; William O. Lamp, Professor, University of Maryland; Arianna Long, Ph.D., University of Washington; Phuong Nguyen, M.D., St. Charles Medical Group; Andy Olesin, B.S., Electrical Engineering; Deborah I. Olszewski, Ph.D., University of Pennsylvania; Akiko Shinya, Chief Fossil Preparator, The Field Museum; Deanna Soper, Ph.D., University of Dallas.

Many thanks also to WonderLab Group (project manager); Grace Hill Smith (project editor); Maya Myers, Ruth Musgrave, and Tonya Grant (writers); Katie Cederborg (fact-checker); Susan K. Hom (proofreader); and Photo Affairs (picture research) for their invaluable help with this book. Special thanks to Sara Lynn Cramb for the many illustrations she created for this project.

Book team: Marfé Ferguson Delano, executive editor; Lori Epstein, photo manager; Mike McNey, map production; Alix Inchausti, senior production editor; Yogi Carroll, production manager; Lauren Sciortino, associate designer.

Printed in South Korea
25/QPSK/1